CW00322122

Rome

Italy

EVERYMAN
CITY GUIDES

EVERYMAN CITY GUIDES

ISBN 1-85715-884-9

First published April 1999

Originally published in France by Nouveaux Loisirs, a subsidiary of Gallimard, Paris 1998, and in Italy by Touring Editore, Srl., Milano 1998.

SERIES EDITORS
Seymourina Cruse/Marisa Bassi
ROME EDITION: Sophie Lenormand (France), Marta Del Zanna, Marina Forlizzi, Fabio Pelliccia (Italy)
GRAPHICS
Élizabeth Cohat, Yann Le Duc
LAYOUT: Silvia Pecora
MINI-MAPS:
Riccardo De Checchi
AIRPORT MAPS:
Kristoff Chemineau
MAPS OF THE AREA:
Édigraphie
STREET MAPS:
Touring Club Italiano
PRODUCTION
Catherine Bourrabier

Translated by Simon Knight and typeset by The Write Idea in association with First Edition Translations Ltd, Cambridge, UK

Printed in Italy by Editoriale Lloyd

Authors Aller & Retour
ROME

Things you need to know: Luca Giannini (1)

L. Giannini took an Art degree and for years has been writing tourist guides and travel books. Though he hails from Milan, his enthusiasm for Rome knows no bounds and he visits the city whenever he can.

Where to stay and **Where to eat:** Stefano Milioni (2)

A journalist and writer specializing in gastronomy and travel, for fifteen years S. Milioni wrote the 'Restaurants' column in the Rome daily *Il Messaggero*. He has contributed to the Italian edition of the *Gault Millau* guide and to many magazines: *Epoca, A Tavola, Tuttoturismo, Gambero Rosso, Vini & Liquori* and *Bar Giornale*. He has lived in Rome since 1975.

After dark: Luca Neri (3)

Journalist, designer and globe-trotter, L. Neri divides his time between Rome and New York. For years he has contributed articles to the weekly *L'Espresso* and such prestigious international publications as *Colors, Vogue, Lei, Per Lui, Glamour* and *Casa Vogue*.

What to see and **Further afield:** Carla Compostella (4)

A native of Rome, C. Compostella holds a diploma in archeology from the University of Milan, where she lives and works. She has written studies on portraiture, culture and iconography in Roman art and has organized a number of exhibitions. An outstanding guide, she will open your eyes to the city of Rome and its surroundings.

Where to shop: Caren Davidkhanian (5)

An Iranian educated in Britain and the United States, C. Davidkhanian has lived in Rome for over fifteen years and is editor-in-chief of the *Italian Press Digest*. He has written the 'Shopping' chapter in the *Sweet Rome* guide and shopping and curiosities columns for the *Daily American, International Daily News* and *International Courier*.

Note from the publisher:
To keep the price of this guide as low as possible we decided on a common edition for the UK and US which has meant American spelling.

Things you need to know ➥ 6

Where to stay ➥ 16

Where to eat ➥ 42

After dark ➥ 72

What to see ➥ 88

Further afield ➥ 122

Where to shop ➥ 138

Finding your way ➥ 164

Symbols

- ☎ telephone
- fax
- ● price or price range
- opening hours
- credit cards accepted
- credit cards not accepted
- toll-free number
- @ e-mail/website address
- ★ tips and recommendations

Access

- subway stations
- bus (or tram)
- private parking
- parking attendant
- no facilities for the disabled
- train
- car
- boat

Hotels

- telephone in room
- fax in room on request
- minibar
- television in room
- air-conditioned rooms
- 24-hour room service
- caretaker
- babysitting
- meeting room(s)
- no pets
- breakfast
- open for tea/coffee
- restaurant
- live music
- disco
- garden, patio or terrace
- gym, fitness club
- swimming pool, sauna

Restaurants

- vegetarian food
- view
- formal dress required
- smoking area
- bar

Museums and galleries

- on-site store(s)
- guided tours
- café

Stores

- branches, outlets

The Insider's Guide is made up of **8 sections** each indicated by a different color.

Things you need to know (mauve)
Where to stay (blue)
Where to eat (red)
After dark (pink)
What to see (green)
Further afield (orange)
Where to shop (yellow)
Finding your way (purple)

B Colosseo *Mon., Tu*
9am–1pm ● *10,000 lire*

Practical information is given for each particular establishment: opening times, prices, ways of paying, different services available

How to use this guide

In the area
In this area are some of the most g
period and three Christian sanctuai

→ 78
■ Where to

The section **"In the area"** refers you (→ 00) to other establishments that are covered in a different section of the guide but found in the same area of the city.

Colosseum **E** B-C 3-4

The small map shows all the establishments mentioned and others described elsewhere but found "in the area", by the color of the section.

The name of the district is given above the map. A grid reference (**A** B-C 2) enables you to find it in the section on Maps at the end of the book.

The section "Not forgetting" lists other useful addresses in the same area.

Not forgetting
■ **San Pietro in Vincoli (40)**
00184 Rome ☎ (06) 4882865 *As we*

"Bargain!"
This star marks good value hotels and restaurants.

The opening page to each section contains an index ordered alphabetically (Getting there), by subject or by district (After dark) as well as useful addresses and advice.

The section "Things you need to know" covers information on getting to Rome and day-to-day life in the city.

Theme pages introduce a selection of establishments on a given topic.

The "Maps" section of this guide contains 9 street plans of Rome followed by a detailed index.

"Child-care facilities"!
Much as you love your children, when visiting Rome you may want to spend some time alone with your partner. If so, entrust your offspring to ***Gioca e crea*** *via Carducci 4 (Termini) ☎ (06) 4740062 children aged two to ten ⏲ 3–8pm ● 8,000 lire/hour (fixed rates for a minimum of 10 hours).*

Getting there

Before leaving home
For brochures and general information, contact the ***Italian Tourist Office:***
in the UK
1 Princes Street London W1R 8AY
☎ 0171 408 1254
in the USA
630 Park Avenue New York 10111
☎ (212) 245 482

Motorists
You are required to carry a valid driver's license, car registration document, international insurance and green card. If you are not the owner of the vehicle, you will also need an authorization from the registered owner.

Formalities

Visitors from EU countries will need a valid identity card or a passport (an old passport is acceptable up to five years out of date). Unaccompanied minors must have an a parental authorization. Non-EU nationals should seek information from the Italian consular authorities in their home country.
Italian Embassy *Three Kings Yard, London W1Y 2EH ☎ 0171 312 2200*
Italian Embassy *1601 Fuller Street NW, Washington, D.C.☎ (202) 328 5500*
Italian Consulate *690 Park Avenue, NY, 10021 (212) 737 9100*

53 Things you need to Know

National holidays

Capodanno (New Year's Day) Jan. 1
Epifania (Epiphany) Jan. 6
Lunedì dell'Angelo Easter Monday
Festival of the Liberation Apr. 25
Festa del lavoro (Labor Day) May 1
Ferragosto (Assumption) Aug. 15
Ognissanti (All Saints' Day) Nov. 1
Immacolata Concezione (Immaculate Conception) Dec. 8
Natale (Christmas) Dec. 25
Santo Stefano Dec. 26

INDEX A-Z

Basic facts

Rome has two international airports. Leonardo da Vinci (often called Fiumicino from the name of the small port on the coast nearby) is 17 miles from the center of Rome. Ciampino airport, at the foot of the Castelli Romani on the Via Appia, is 9 miles southeast of the city center.

Getting there

Leonardo da Vinci–Fiumicino

Information
☎ *(06) 65953640*
Daily 24 hours

Airport services

Luggage
☎ *(06) 65954252*
Daily 24 hours

Post office
International terminal
☎ *(06) 65010217*
Mon.–Fri. 8am–12.50pm, 1.50–6.50pm; Sat. 8am–12.50pm
National terminal
☎ *(06) 65010612*
Mon.–Fri. 8am–12.50pm, 1.50–6.50pm; Sat. 8am–12.50pm

First aid
☎ *(06) 65953133 or 65953134*
Daily 24 hours

Ente Provinciale per il Turismo
Tourist office
☎ *(06) 65956074 or 65954471*
Mon.–Sat. 8.15am–7.15pm

Car rental

Avis
☎ *(06) 65011531*
Daily 7am–midnight

Eurodollar
☎ *(06) 65953547*
Daily 7am–midnight

Europcar
☎ *(06) 65010879 or 65010977*
Daily 7am–11pm

Hertz
☎ *(06) 5011553*
Mon.–Fri. 7am–midnight; Sat. Sun. 7am–11pm

Maggiore Budget
☎ *(06) 65011508 or 65011678*
Daily 7am–midnight

Fiumicino–Rome connections
➡ 188

Train

Airport–Roma Termini
There is a direct 'FS' (state railways) link with Termini station, with trains leaving every hour. Journey time approx. 30 mins.
Daily 7.50am–10.05pm
● *15,000 lire*

Airport–other stations
The FM1 *ferrovia metropolitana* (suburban railway) line stops at the following stations: Roma Ostiense, Roma Tuscolana, Roma Tiburtina. Trains leave every 20 mins. Journey time: 20 to 40 mins.
Daily 6.28am–0.13am
● *11,400 lire*

Cotral bus
Leaves from outside International Arrivals. Ticket office inside the terminal.
Daily 7am–6.40pm

Airport–Magliana subway station
Connection with subway line B: every hour.
Daily 5.35am–10.25pm
● *4,500 lire*

Airport–Lepanto subway station
Connections with line A: every hour.
Daily 5.30am–7.10pm
● *4,900 lire*

Airport–Roma Tiburtina station
A night time bus service connects the airport with Roma Tiburtina station, where you can transfer to suburban railway line FM2 and subway line B. Buses leave every hour. Buy your ticket on the bus.
Daily 1.15am–5am
● *7,000 lire*

Taxis
Allow 45 mins to city center. Take an official (yellow and white) taxi and check correct charge is showing on meter before you leave.
● *approx. 60,000 lire (add minimum charge of 15,500 lire, and other supplements for luggage, night time and public holiday service).*

Car park
Bus
Train
Car rental

Leonardo da Vinci International Airport **FCC**

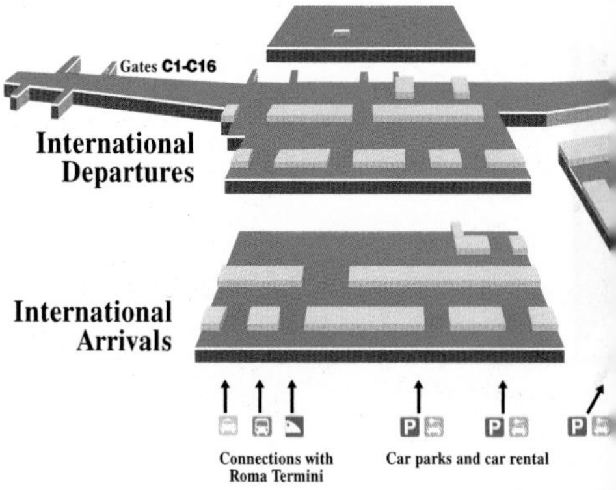

Apart from a few internal services, it is used for charter flights.

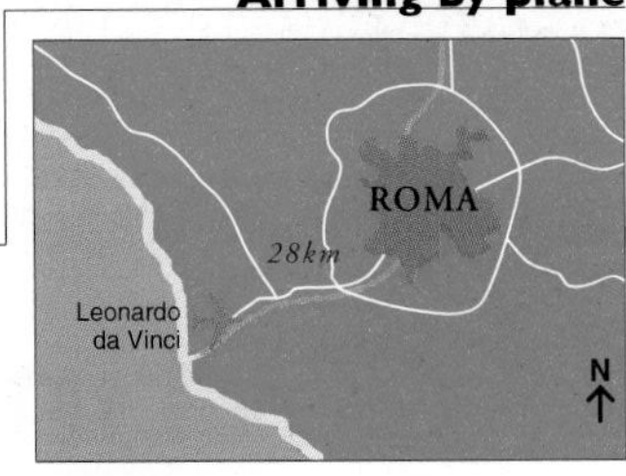

G.B. Pastine-Ciampino airport

Information
☎ (06) 794941
🕒 *Daily 7am–11pm*

Airport services
Luggage
☎ (06) 79494225
🕒 *Daily 7am–11pm*
Post office
☎ (06) 79340104
🕒 *Mon.–Fri. 8am–1.50pm; Sat. 8–11.50am*

Car rental
Avis
☎ (06) 79340195
🕒 *Mon.–Fri. 8am–10pm; Sat. 10am–6pm; Sun. 1–8pm*
Eurodollar
☎ (06) 79340838
🕒 *Mon.–Fri. 8.45am–12.45pm, 2–6.30pm; Sat 8.20am–12.30pm*
Europcar
☎ (06) 79340387
🕒 *Mon.–Fri. 8am–1pm, 2–6pm; Sat. 8am–12 noon*
Hertz
☎ (06) 79340095
🕒 *Mon.–Fri. 8am–12.30pm, 4–7.30pm; Sat. 9am–12.30pm*
Maggiore Budget
☎ (06) 79340368
🕒 *Mon.–Fri. 7.30am–8pm; Sat., Sun. 5–8pm*

Ciampino–Rome connections
➡ 188

Cotral bus
Airport–Ciampino station
There is a regular bus link with the Anagnina subway station (line A). The bus leaves from outside the International Departures area of the terminal, where there is a ticket office and ticket machine (make sure you have change). Journey time: approx. 30 mins.
🕒 *Daily 6.50am–11.40pm*
● *1,500 lire*

Train
FM4 (suburban line) trains leave every 10–15 mins for Roma Termini station. Connections with subway line A.
● *2,000 lire*
🕒 *Daily 6.20am–11.10pm*

Taxis
Allow 30 mins for the journey. Take an official (yellow and white) taxi.
● *approx. 40,000 lire*

Airlines

Alitalia
Via Bissolati, 3
☎ (06) 65621
National and international flight inquiries.
☎ (06) 65643

UK
Alitalia
☎ 0181 745 8200
➟ 0171 602 5584/ 0171 646 0471
British Airways
☎ 0345 222111
Lufthansa
☎ 0345 737747

US
Alitalia
☎ 800 223 5730
American Airlines
☎ 800 433 7300
British Airways
☎ 800 AIRWAYS
Delta
☎ 800 221 1212
TWA
☎ 800 892 4141

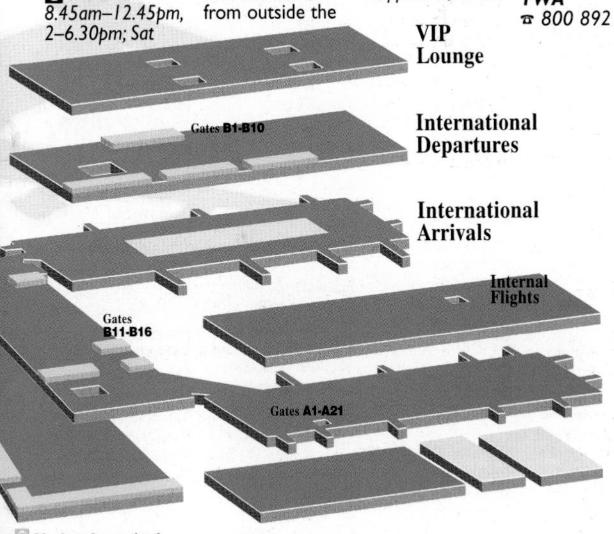

Basic facts

Trains from the north arrive at Roma Termini station (1), right in the heart of the city. To reach your final destination, you can take a bus from the main bus station, which is in the station forecourt. If you are arriving by car, buy a Viacard (2), so as to avoid the lines at motorway toll-booths.

Getting there

1

2

Arriving by train

This is not the ideal way to arrive in Rome, as most journeys from London take over twenty-four hours. The most comfortable itinerary is to travel by Eurostar from London to Lille, then take the direct TGV service to Dijon and try to connect with an overnight train to Rome. Alternatively, go via Lyons to Milan and take a high-speed Pendolino to Rome. After a good night's sleep, you can view the Italian countryside while enjoying a *cappuccino*. Take some local currency, as meals in the restaurant car have to be paid for in cash. The cost of round-trip tickets varies considerably depending on the type of trains chosen.

Information, reservations
UK:
Rail Europe Travel Centre,
179 Picadilly,
London W1
☎ *0990 848 848*
US:
CIT Tours (official representative of Italian State Railroads),
342 Madison Avenue, New York 10173
℡ *800 223 7987*
Italy:
℡ 1478 88088
⏲ *Daily, 7am–9pm*

Roma Termini central station

Piazzale dei Cinquecento
☎ *(06) 4775*
Most national and international trains arrive at Roma Termini station ➡ 102, which is on the edge of the *centro storico* (the historic heart of the city). The various districts are served by Rome's two subway lines (A and B, map ➡ 188) and by many buses. The bus station is in the station forecourt.

Reservations
☎ *(06) 47306250*
⏲ *Daily 24 hours*
Left luggage
☎ *(06) 47306275*
⏲ *Daily 5.20am–0.20am*
Lost property
☎ *(06) 47306682*
⏲ *Daily 7am–11pm*

Station facilities
Bureau de change
⏲ *Daily 24 hours*
Hotel information
☎ *(06) 4871270*
⏲ *Mon.–Sat. 8.15am–7.15pm*
Car rental
Maggiore
☎ *(06) 4880049*
⏲ *Mon.–Fri. 7am–7.45pm; Sat. 7am–6pm; Sun. 8.30am–12.30pm*
Hertz
☎ *(06) 4740389*
⏲ *Mon.–Sat. 7am–8pm*
Avis
☎ *(06) 4814373*
⏲ *Mon.–Fri. 7am–8pm; Sat. 8am–6pm; Sun. 8am–1pm*

Roma Tiburtina station

Circonvallazione Nomentana
☎ *(06) 44245104*
Night trains from Milan, Florence and the South (Reggio di Calabria, Palermo) tend to arrive at this station, which

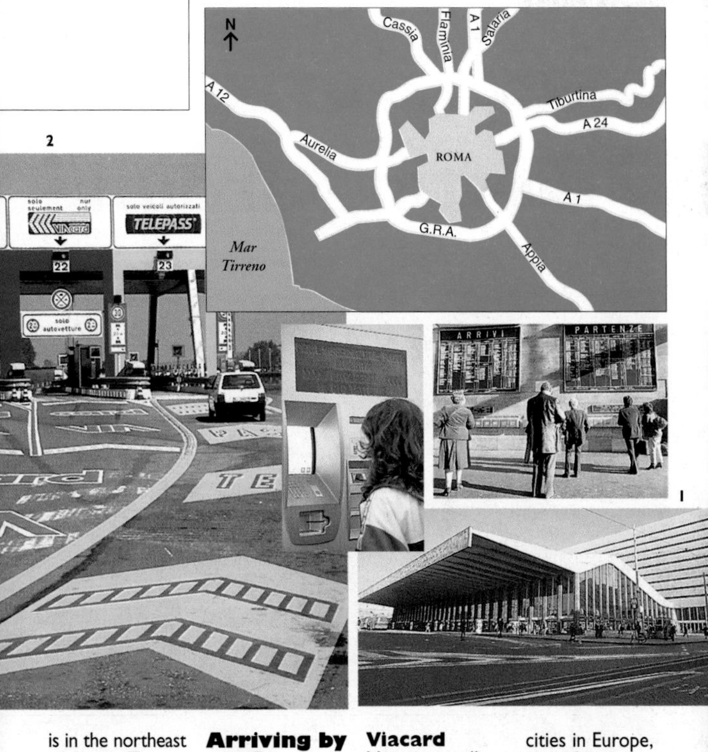

2

1

is in the northeast of the city. To reach the *centro storico*, take subway line B, or one of the buses which leave from the station forecourt. For Roma Ostiense station, take *ferrovia metropolitana* (suburban railway) line FM1 (Orte–Fiumicino).

Roma Ostiense station

Piazzale dei Partigiani
☎ *(06) 57507320*
In the west of the city, this station is the terminus for trains arriving from northwest Italy (Genoa, Turin, etc.). It is connected to the city center by subway line B and various bus services.

Arriving by road

From the Channel ports, the best route is via the Mont Blanc tunnel. Rome is connected to the main Italian cities by a good motorway network. The most important of these *autostrade* are the A1 (*Autostrada del Sole, Milan–Naples*), the A12 (*Rome–Civitavecchia*) and the A24 (*Rome–L'Aquila*). To see more of the countryside, take the older national routes: the Via Aurelia (*Grosseto–Civitavecchia*); the Appia (*Naples–Formia*); the Cassia (*Siena–Viterbo*), the Flaminia (*Terni–Spoleto*) and the Tiburtina (*Pescara–Avezzano*)

Viacard

Motorway tolls must be paid in cash or by Viacard. These cards can be purchased for 50,000 or 100,000 lire at Italian service stations or toll-booths.

Speed limits

Speed limits in Italy are: 80 mph on motorways, 56 mph on main national highways, and 30 mph in built-up areas.

Breakdown services

Automobile Club Italiano (ACI)
☎ *116*

Bus services

Eurolines runs services to Roma Tiburtina station from all the major cities in Europe, apart from Switzerland. Journey times from London are between thirty-three and thirty-five hours, depending on the date of departure.

Eurolines
52 Grosvenor Gardens, London SW1
☎ *0171 730 8235*
Information and reservations
Mon.–Fri. 9am–5.30pm; Sat. 9am–4pm
● Round trip: London–Rome £125–£135, $202–$218; reductions for travelers under 25 years old or over 60.

Basic facts

Traffic is restricted in many of Rome's streets (1) and parking regulated (2) or completely banned. There are several kinds of ticket (3) for use on public transport (4). The inset map shows the most convenient bus routes for getting around the city center.

Getting around

1

3

4

Subway

Map ➡ ***188***
Information
📞 *167431784 (in Italian)*
🕒 *Mon.–Sat. 8am–8pm*
Although there are only two lines, this is the quickest and cheapest way of getting across town. Subway entrances are marked by a white 'M' on a red background. Line A (red) crosses the city from northwest to southeast, line B (blue) from northeast to southwest.
🕒 *Trains run from 5.30am–11.30pm*
● *1,500 lire, ticket valid for a single journey.*

Buses, streetcars

Map ➡ ***188***
These are part of the ATAC transport network.
Information
Piazzale dei Cinquecento (in front of Roma Termini station)
☎ *(06) 46954444*
Stops are indicated by yellow panels showing the route, timetable and connections.
🕒 *5am–1am*
Thirty or so buses run throughout the night. These are indicated by an 'N' after the route number.

Tickets

Cannot be purchased on the bus, except at night. They are on sale at tobacconists and news-stands, and from vending machines. Be warned: the machines do not always give you your change.
● *1,500 lire, ticket valid for 75 mins; 6,000 lire for a day ticket (Biglietto Integrato Giornaliero, or BIG), also valid for subway rides; 24,000 lire for a weekly ticket (Carta Integrata Settimanale, or CIS), also valid for the subway.*

COTRAL

Map ➡ ***188***
Three suburban railway lines, leaving from Ostiense, Laziali and Flaminio railway stations.

Taxis

The yellow and white official taxis can be hailed in the street or boarded at the head of a taxi rank. Make sure the fare meter is showing only the minimum charge before you set off. To pre-book a taxi, refer to the *Pagine Gialle* (Yellow Pages) under 'Taxi'.
Radiotaxis
☎ *(06) 3570; (06) 4994; (06) 6645; (06) 5551*
● *4,500 lire for the first two miles or the first nine minutes. There are*

surcharges for luggage, night journeys (10pm–7am) and public holidays.

Driving in Rome

Traffic is heavy and journeys are often disrupted by events of a public nature (strikes, papal appearances, visiting heads of state, etc.). The entire central district, or *fascia blu* (blue zone), is off limits to traffic from 6.30am to 6pm Monday to Friday and 2 to 6pm on Saturdays. This includes the streets in the triangle formed by the Piazza del Popolo, the Piazza Colonna and the Piazza Barberini.

Parking
In the city center and adjacent areas you have to pay to park, and in any case parking is restricted to night time and public holidays. Parking meters accept 100, 200 and 500 lire coins, or plastic cards which can be purchased at news-stands and tobacconists.
● *2, 000 lire/hour*

Car parks
Near subway stations there are *parcheggi di scambio* ('transfer car parks'), where you can leave your car and continue by public transport. It is cheaper to pay by the day.
● *2, 000 lire/day*

Main 'parcheggi di scambio'
Subway line A: Piazza di Spagna-Villa Borghese; Anagnina, Colli Albani-via Albano; Arco di Travertino; Cinecittà.
Subway line B: Ponte Mammolo; Tiburtina; Garbatella; EUR Magliana; Laurentina.

Bicycles

Built on seven hills, Rome is not the ideal place for cyclists, even the most experienced. The districts most suited to a relaxed bike ride are those between the Villa Borghese, the banks of the Tiber, the Piazza Navona and the Pantheon.

Collalti
Via del Pellegrino 80/82
☎ *(06) 68801084*
● *15,000 lire/day.*

Scooters

The famous Vespas of the 1950s and ubiquitous *motorini* (noisy little motorcycles) are an excellent way of getting around the city center. You are advised to wear a helmet.

Scoot-a-long
Via Cavour 302
☎ *(06) 6780206*
● *70,000 lire/day.*

Basic facts

An agreeably nostalgic way of seeing the sights of Rome is to hire a horse-drawn carriage. The cost is 60,000 lire per hour, leaving from Piazza di Spagna, Piazza Navona, the Trevi Fountain, the Coliseum or St. Peter's Square.

Getting by

Money

Italians generally pay cash. Some businesses, such as family-run restaurants (*trattorie*) and shops, do not accept credit cards.

Currency
The unit of currency is the Italian lira (plural: lire). Notes come in 1,000, 2,000, 5,000, 10,000, 50,000, 100,000 and 500,000 lire denominations. There are also 50, 100, 200, 500 and 1,000 lire coins.

Banks
Mon.–Fri. 8.30am–1.30pm, 2.45–3.45pm
However, these times vary from bank to bank, and some of the big banks also open on Saturday mornings. When changing foreign currency, you will usually get a more favorable rate at a bank than at a *bureau de change*.

Bureaux de change
£1 = c. 2,800 lire; US$1 = c. 1,780 lire. There are many *bureaux de change* around Roma Termini station and in the districts most frequented by tourists (St. Peter's, Piazza di Spagna, Via Veneto). The advantage is that they are open late into the evening and on public holidays.

Cash dispensers
There are Bancomat machines in most areas. In the event of a problem, contact:
Visa-Marstercard
☎ *167821001*
Amex
☎ *(06) 72280735*

Tipping
Round up your bill, adding at least 10%.

The Media

Roman daily papers
Il Messagero; La Repubblica; Il Tempo; Il Corriere dello Sport
Most of the main national dailies devote several pages to specifically Roman news. On Thursdays *La Repubblica* publishes *Trovaroma*, a useful supplement with information about entertainment in Rome.

International newspapers
News-stands in the city center sell a wide range of foreign newspapers. Traditionally, those on the Via Veneto have the best selection.

Radio
Short-wave transistor radios can pick up broadcasts from the BBC, Voice of America and CBC (Canadian programs)

Television
Italy's public-service channels are RAI Uno, Due and Tre. Many European channels can be received via cable, as can CNN International news network.

Bookstores

Most of the large bookstores stock a wide range of English-language titles.
Libreria internazionale
Via Tomacelli, 144
☎ *(06) 68808160*

Telephone

Local calls
Dial the number you require, without the 06 code.

National calls
Dial the city code (Rome 06, Milan 02), then the number.

International calls
Calling Rome
From the UK, dial

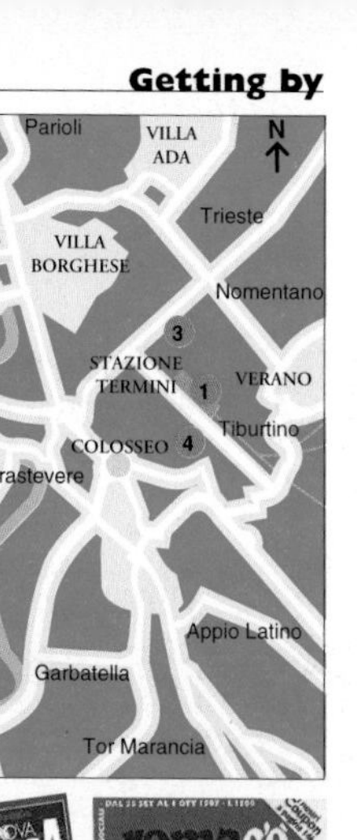

00-39-06, followed by the number. From the USA., dial 011-39-06, followed by the number.

Calling a foreign country
Dial 00, followed by the country code, city code and number.

International inquiries
☎ 176

Collect calls
☎ 170

Telecom agencies
For inter-city and international calls.

Stazione Roma Termini (1)
🕓 *Daily 8am–10pm*

Public telephones
Easily identified by their bright orange color, public telephones accept 100, 200 and 500 lire coins, as well as *gettoni* (tokens) and phone cards bought at tobacconists' shops, in post offices and in some bars. In central Rome there are a number of calling centers from which you can make calls abroad at reduced rates.

Postal services

🕓 *Mon.–Fri. 8.30am–1.50pm; Sat. 8.30am–12.50pm; post offices close at 11.40am on the last day of the month.*

Roma Prati main post office (2)
Viale Giuseppe Mazzini 101
☎ *(06) 37517611 or 37516561*
All services: *poste restante* (*Fermo Posta*), express (*Postacelere*), fax, etc.
🕓 *Mon.–Fri. 8am–6pm; Sat. and last day of month 8am–2pm*

Vatican postal services
Cost the same as Italian national services, but is quicker. Mail must be stamped with Vatican postage stamps and mailed in a blue 'Poste Vaticane' box.

Tourist offices

Ente Provinciale per il Turismo di Roma (EPT) (3)
Via Parigi 11
☎ *(06) 488991*
🕓 *Mon.–Sat. 8.15am–7.15pm*
Termini station
🕓 *Daily 8.15am–7.15pm*

Ente Nazionale Italiano per il Turismo (ENIT) (4)
Via Marghera 2/6
☎ *(06) 49711*
🕓 *Mon.–Fri. 9am–5.30pm*

Ufficio Informazioni Pellegrini e Turisti (5)
Piazza San Pietro
☎ *(06) 69884466*
🕓 *Mon.–Sat. 8.30am–7pm*

Guide e Corrieri turistici
Via Parigi 11
☎ *(06) 488991*

Embassies

Canada
Via B. Oriani 61
☎ *(06) 68307316*

UK
Via XX Settembre, 80 A
☎ *(06) 4825441*

USA
Via Vittorio Veneto, 119 A
☎ *(06) 46741*

Emergency services

Polizia (emergency)
☎ *113*

Polizia Stradale (traffic police)
☎ *(06) 5544194*

Questura (prefecture)
☎ *(06) 4686*

Carabinieri (armed police)
☎ *112*

Vigili del Fuoco (fire service)
☎ *115*

Polizia Municipale
☎ *(06) 67691*

Emergenza sanitaria (SAMU)
☎ *118*

Where to stay

Youth hostels

Ostello per la Gioventù 'A.F. Pessina'
Viale delle Olimpiadi 61 (Foro Italico)
☎ *(06) 3236267*

YWCA
For women only.
Via Cesare Balbo 4 (Termini)
☎ *(06) 460460*

Centro accoglienza Giovanni XXIII
For foreign students.
Lungotevere dei Vallati 1 (near the Ghetto) ☎ *(06) 6864460*

Prices and services
The following information is given for each hotel: number of rooms; price range of a double room; number of suites; cost of breakfast (continental); facilities.

64 Hotels

THE INSIDER'S FAVORITES

Book in advance!
A popular destination all year round, Rome does not really have a low season. You are therefore advised to book before you leave home, especially between July and September. If you arrive without a reservation, you can inquire at the hotel reservations office at Fiumicino airport or Roma Termini station. A factor to consider is that many hotels are being renovated in preparation for the millennium Jubilee.
Hotel reservations *☎ (06) 6991000*
⏲ 7am–10pm

Convents
One possibility to consider is staying in a convent. Men and women are often segregated, however, and gates are closed between 10 and 11pm.
Pastoral reception center
Via Santa Giovanna d'Arco 10
☎ (06) 68803815

INDEX BY PRICE

5 LEVELS OF HOTEL PRICES
● less than 250,000 lire
● ● 251,000–350,000 lire
● ● ● 351,000–450,000 lire
● ● ● ● 451,000–600,000 lire
● ● ● ● ● more than 600,000 lire

In the area

It is undoubtedly in the northern area of the city, between Termini station and Porta Pia, that the Roman hotel industry has made the greatest strides in recent years. Prices are reasonable, and there is now no need to sacrifice comfort or put up with poor service in order to

Where to stay

Artdeco (1)

Via Palestro 19 – 00185 Rome
☎ (06) 4457588 ➠ (06) 4441483

M *B Castro Pretorio* P ***35 rooms ●●●*** *14 suites* @ *artdeco@uni.net*

A hotel with a difference, with décor as elegant as the name suggests. The sophisticated atmosphere and original features, together with a high level of service, place this hotel in the above-average category. Most of the attractive bathrooms are equipped with hydro-massage baths or showers. A buffet-style breakfast is served in the delightful roof-top garden.

Andreotti (2)

Via Castelfidardo 55 – 00185 Rome
☎ (06) 4441301 ➠ (06) 4453777

M *B Castro Pretorio* ***55 rooms ●●*** *1 suite*

The management of this hotel see it as their mission to ensure the peace and well-being of their guests, employing attentive staff and taking great care with the decoration. The rooms were completely refurbished a few years ago, and the functional bathrooms show a similar concern for detail. ★ Several are equipped with sauna-showers, a definite plus for those who enjoy this form of pampering.

Marghera (3)

Via Marghera 29 – 00185 Rome
☎ (06) 4457679 / 4450769 / 4457184 ➠ (06) 4462539

M *A, B Termini* P ***25 rooms ●●***

Cross the threshold and you will find it hard to believe the railroad station is only fifty yards away. The décor is enlivened with touches of bright color; there are cut flowers in every room; and soft pillows and spotless towels give a real sense of comfort and exclusivity. Every detail expresses the owners' concern to make each guest feel at home in an attractive setting. Purely practical considerations are also taken into account. The spacious rooms, which have immaculate bathrooms, are all equipped with trouser presses.

Not forgetting

■ **Galles (4)** Viale del Castro Pretorio 66 – 00185 Rome ☎ (06) 4454741 ➠ (06) 4456993 ●●●●● *Interesting rooms, some on two levels. Some of the beautifully designed bathrooms are fitted with jacuzzis.*
■ **Venezia (5)** Via Varese 18 – 00185 Rome ☎ (06) 4457101 ➠ (06) 4957687 ● *Maybe the cleanliness of this hotel reflects the Swiss origins of its owner! An intelligent pricing policy, smiling staff, efficient service, attractively furnished public areas and quiet rooms.*

enjoy the advantages of a district which is well served by public transport.

1

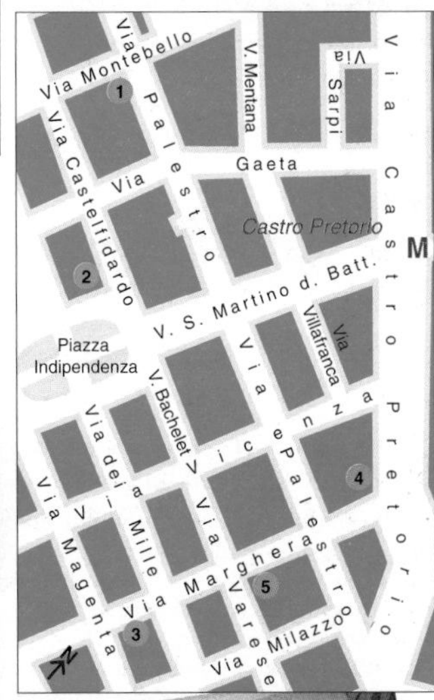

1

1

5

5

In the area

In the heyday of railroad travel, before the advent of airplanes, the major hotels were situated near train stations. This explains the concentration of imposing 19th-century establishments just south of Termini station ➡ 102, between the Piazza della Repubblica and Via Cavour.

Where to stay

Le Grand Hotel (6)

Via V.E. Orlando 3 – 00185 Rome ☎ (06) 47091 ➡ (06) 4747307

M *A Repubblica* ***134 rooms*** ●●●●● *36 suites* *30,000 lire*

As you enter the Grand, you are following in the footsteps of many famous people who, for more than a century, have trod its thick carpets, walked in the bright light of its Murano crystal chandeliers, and met their friends under its high frescoed ceilings. You are bound to come under the spell of its turn-of-the-century atmosphere and luxuriously appointed public rooms. The bedrooms are decorated in varying styles. You may be lucky enough to sleep in an antique bed and read by the light of an authentic Venetian table lamp.

Massimo d'Azeglio (7)

Via Cavour 18 – 00184 Rome ☎ (06) 4880646 ➡ (06) 4827386

M *A, B Termini* ***210 rooms*** ●●● *167-860004* @ *bettoja@uni.net*

You could hardly claim that this hotel was situated in a nice quiet street. Yet this is a hotel of character, and highly convenient if you are in Rome for a brief stay or visiting the city for the first time. The decoration of its lounges, bedrooms and meeting rooms gives a true sense of 19th-century elegance, which more than makes up for the hubbub of the busy city. A better bet than international hotels of similar size and standard.

Mecenate Palace Hotel (8)

Via Carlo Alberto 3 – 00185 Rome
☎ (06) 44702024 ➡ (06) 4461354

M *A Repubblica* ***59 rooms*** ●●●● *3 suites* @ *mecenate@venere.it*

After a bold refurbishment, this little *palazzo* is a sheer delight. Beautiful rooms, elegant, warm and welcoming; spacious, comfortable bathrooms, whose luxurious marble beats even the most attractive ceramic tiles.
★ Go up to the roof terrace for a fine view of the city, and why not try the fare in the hotel's own, very pleasant restaurant?

Not forgetting

■ **Impero (9)** Via del Viminale 19 – 00184 Rome ☎ (06) 4820067 ➡ (06) 4837762 ●●●●● *Recommended for the friendly atmosphere of its public areas, large and small lounges, reading room and veranda, and for the happy marriage of tradition and modernity in its décor.*

■ **Viminale (10)** Via Balbo 31 – 00184 Rome ☎ (06) 4881980 ➡ (06) 4872018 ●●●●● *The attractions of this former headquarters of the Compagnie des Wagons-lits are the courtesy of its staff; its silent, fabric-hung rooms, some graced with Liberty furniture; and its pleasant roof-top dining room.*

■ **Britannia (11)** Via Napoli 64 – 00184 Rome ☎ (06) 4883153 ➡ (06) 4882343 ●● *Entirely refurbished in contemporary style. Comfort and good service. Full English breakfast. Car park free, but closed at night.*

Where to eat ➥ 46
After dark ➥ 74
What to see ➥ 102
Where to shop ➥ 140

7

8

11

8

8

In the area
The *dolce vita* is only a memory and the stars have deserted the Via Vittorio Veneto. All that remains are the hotels which formed the backdrop to their showy lifestyle. Still, they have retained their splendor and an atmosphere of worldly sophistication, combining luxury with practicality. ■ After dark

Where to stay

Excelsior (12)

Via V. Veneto 125 – 00187 Rome ☎ (06) 47081 ➠ (06) 4826205

M *A Barberini* ***282 rooms*** ●●●●● *45 suites*

This was for many years a favorite haunt of film stars. Nowadays it draws its clientele from a wider social spectrum, but has retained something of its former Hollywood glamour. There is a degree of theatricality in its sumptuous décor and excellent service.

De La Ville (13)

Via Sistina 69 – 00187 Rome ☎ (06) 67331 ➠ (06) 6784213

M *A Spagna* ***169 rooms*** ●●●●● *23 suites*

Neoclassical in its architecture and furnishings, this hotel occupies a dominant position, almost at the top of Trinità dei Monti hill. From the sun lounge and top-floor rooms, there is a magnificent view over the city below.

Eden (14)

Via Ludovisi 49 – 00187 Rome ☎ (06) 478121 ➠ (06) 4821584

M *A Barberini* ***101 rooms*** ●●●●● *11 suites* *34 000 LIT* *1678-20088*

For more than a century, this venerable institution has been welcoming opera singers, film directors and royalty. After a face-lift that has not detracted from its original style, in 1994 the Eden reopened its doors and reclaimed its position as one of the world's great hotels. Its exclusive, old-fashioned charm is the product of its sophisticated atmosphere, sumptuous decoration and antique furniture, vast bedrooms – all different, with marble bathrooms – panoramic restaurant and piano bar. ★ The hotel lays on chauffeur-driven cars for its patrons – a nice little extra! The welcome you receive is on a par with the setting: truly delightful.

Dei Borgognoni (15)

Via del Bufalo 126 – 00187 Rome
☎ (06) 69941505 / 6780041 ➠ (06) 69941501

M *A Spagna* P ***50 rooms*** ●●●●

Hidden away in a 17th-century *palazzo*, this hotel exemplifies a genius for discretion, as well as the well-known Roman love of luxury. Quiet atmosphere and warm welcome.

Not forgetting

■ **Barocco (16)** Piazza Barberini 9 – 00187 Rome ☎ (06) 4872001 ➠ (06) 485994 ●●● *Small and intimate, the ideal place if you are looking for comfort without ostentation.* ■ **Scalinata di Spagna (17)** Piazza della Trinità dei Monti 17 – 00187 Rome ☎ (06) 6793006 ➠ (06) 69940598 ●●● *Tucked away at the top of the Spanish Steps. Breakfast on the terrace with a fine view over the city.*

➥ 74 ➥ 80 ➥ 86 ■ What to see ➥ 110 ➥ 114 ■ What to buy ➥ 162

In the area

At first sight you might not expect to find hotels in this district of shopping streets and quiet residential blocks. However a number of large hotels, and some less expensive ones, are hidden away in the triangle bounded by the Via del Tritone and the streets which fan out from the Piazza del Popolo.

Where to stay

Hotel d'Inghilterra (18)

Via Bocca di Leone 14 – 00187 Rome ☎ (06) 69981 ➟ (06) 69922243

M *A Spagna* P ***112 rooms* ●●●●** *8 suites* *167-010058*

Set back from the roadway in a pedestrianized street, this former annex of Palazzo Torlonia has all the charm and distinction of a 15th-century aristocratic residence. As soon as it opened, in 1850, it attracted royalty, artists and celebrities such as Liszt and Hemingway. It certainly lives up to its past, with a magnificent black-and-white marble lobby, period furniture, Persian carpets, a collection of Neapolitan paintings, fine pictures and prints, as well as first-class service. The bedrooms, which are larger on the fourth and fifth floors, are individually decorated.

Plaza (19)

Via del Corso 126 – 00186 Rome ☎ (06) 69921111 ➟ (06) 69941575

M *A Spagna* ***186 rooms* ●●●●●** *9 suites* @ *plaza@italyhotel.com*

Although unusually large for a city-center hotel, the Plaza has a relaxed, peaceful atmosphere. There is a splendid rococo staircase in the main lobby. The bedrooms are of a good standard, though perhaps a little old-fashioned.

Valadier (20)

Via della Fontanella 15 – 00187 Rome
☎ (06) 3610592 / 3612344 / 3611998 ➟ (06) 3201558

M *A Flaminio* ***41 rooms* ●●●●** *4 suites* @ *valadier@venere.it*

This little hotel, hidden away in a quiet street, is the ideal refuge for those of a romantic disposition. A minor masterpiece of interior decoration, with wooden paneling and Persian carpets on the marble floors.

Carriage (21)

Via delle Carrozze 36 – 00187 Rome ☎ (06) 6990124 ➟ (06) 6788279

M *A Spagna* ***22 rooms* ●●** *2 suites*

Delicate pastel shades, the luxury of fine building materials, and large flower arrangements. This little hotel is a real haven of peace and civility. ★ When you arrive, ask for one of the two rooms with a terrace (n° 501 or n° 601). They cannot be reserved in advance. Failing this, when the weather is fine, you can always have your breakfast on the roof terrace rather than in the pleasant ground-floor dining room.

Not forgetting

■ **Croce di Malta (22)** Via Borgognona 28 – 00187 Rome ☎ (06) 6795482 / 69940250 ➟ (06) 780675 ●● *Spacious, soundproofed bedrooms and functional bathrooms.*

■ **Locarno (23)** Via della Penna 22 – 00186 Rome ☎ (06) 3610841/2/3 ➟ (06) 3215249 ●● *A charming hotel with a turn-of-the-century atmosphere. Its unusual features include literary evenings and loan of bicycles, open fires and a patio garden.*

- Where to eat ➥ 48 ➥ 52
- After dark ➥ 84
- What to see ➥ 110
- Where to shop ➥ 144 ➥ 146

The Hotel Valadier is named after architect and town planner Giuseppe Valadier (1762–1839), who was responsible for laying out the Piazza del Popolo, one of the city's largest squares.

20

19

23

19

In the area
Many embassies are located in the chic Parioli district, particularly in the attractive area adjacent to the Villa Borghese. Nestling in the greenery among the patrician villas are a number of luxury hotels with an air of quiet sophistication. ■ What to see ➡ 112

Where to stay

Lord Byron (24)

Via de Notaris 5 – 00197 Rome
☎ (06) 3224541 ➡ (06) 3220405

52, 926 Viale Buozzi ***30 rooms***
●●●● *7 suites*
Le Relais du Jardin

Regarded by many as Rome's finest hotel, the Lord Byron is only a stone's throw from the Villa Giulia and the Galleria d'Arte Moderna ➡ 112. It is a small building with a 1920s atmosphere, the owner having preserved the feeling of a luxurious private residence. White is the dominant color. Immaculate façade, discreetly picked out in black; harmonious blinds in matching tones; gloss-painted ceilings setting off comfortable armchairs marked with the house emblem; immaculate linen. The rather simple rooms are perhaps the only weakness. ★ The hotel's restaurant, the Relais du Jardin, has for many years been popular with Roman diners and with professional gourmets.

Aldrovandi Palace (25)

Via Aldrovandi 15 – 00197 Rome
☎ (06) 3223993 ➡ (06) 3221435

19 Via Aldrovandi ***122 rooms***
●●●●● *15 suites*
Le Relais de la Piscine
hotel@aldrovandi.com

Formerly a college for the sons of the wealthy, this is now one of the world's most prestigious hotels. In its public rooms, highly polished antique furniture reflects the light cast by crystal chandeliers, while wooden paneling and luxurious carpets add a warmer note. In the bedrooms, shades of pink and pastel green create a softer environment. Set in a park opposite the Villa Borghese ➡ 112, the hotel is a little world of its own, with tennis court and a swimming pool overlooked by a very pleasant restaurant, the Relais de la Piscine.

25

25

27

26

Elegance and outstanding quality of service in a unique setting: the magnificent park created in the 17th century by Cardinal Scipione Borghese.

24

24

Parco dei Principi (26)

Via Frescobaldi 5 – 00198 Rome
☎ (06) 854421 ➡ (06) 8845104

19 Viale Rossini *161 rooms* ●●●●● *14 suites*

This hotel, designed in the 1960s by architect Giò Ponti, has recently emerged from a long period of lethargy, its reputation restored after a refurbishment. The rooms now come up to the highest standards of comfort, where previously their main attraction was the view. The windows look out onto private gardens and, from the rooms on the top floor, the view extends from the Villa Borghese ➡ 112 as far as St Peter's ➡ 108.

Not forgetting

■ **Villa Borghese (27)** Via Pinciana 31 – 00198 Rome ☎ (06) 85300919 ➡ (06) 8414100 ●●● *Though not large, the rooms are comfortable and furnished in good taste. The atmosphere is friendly. Just over the road is the park of the Villa Borghese, a green enclave in the heart of the city.*

In the area

The residential Parioli district is gradually being taken over by office accommodation. Hotels have moved in, eager to meet the needs of business travelers attracted by the quiet environment and the convenient location. ■ Where to eat ➥ 50 ■ Where to shop ➥ 148

Where to stay

Degli Aranci (28)

Via B. Oriani 11 – 00197 Rome ☎ / ➥ (06) 8070202

919, 926 Via Siacci **52 rooms ●●** *2 suites*

This is a good hotel for people who, when evening comes, prefer to withdraw after a hard day and relax in comfortable surroundings without frills. The Aranci is a haven of peace, offering modern, clean, convenient accommodation. The public areas have more character, for instance the pleasant breakfast room which overlooks an orchard of orange trees. Unfortunately, the garden is usually closed to residents. ★ Excellent quality/price ratio.

Polo (29)

Piazza B. Gastaldi 4 – 00197 Rome
☎ (06) 3221041 ➥ (06) 3221359

52, 926 Viale Buozzi **66 rooms ●●●**
polo@networld.it

Built in the 1980s, the Polo has achieved a successful balance between elegance and functionality. Carefully thought out in every detail, the contemporary decoration of its huge bedrooms creates a slightly colonial atmosphere.

Borromini (30)

Via Lisbona 7 – 00197 Rome ☎ (06) 8841321 ➥ (06) 8417550

4, 19 Piazza Ungheria **84 rooms ●●●** *6 suites*

Adjacent to the Villa Ada, in a quiet, leafy area, this is a hotel complex of the highest standard. However, you will not find the slightly old-fashioned charm characteristic of many venerable Roman institutions. Everything is planned to satisfy the needs of an international business clientele. For instance, the Borromini offers many services and the technical equipment needed for holding conferences and seminars. The spacious bedrooms, some with terrace, are attractively decorated.

Not forgetting

■ **Rivoli (31)** Via T. Taramelli 7 – 00197 Rome ☎ (06) 3224333 ➥ (06) 3227373 ●● *Prices fully justified by the services on offer. Garden, pleasant lounges, and large rooms with stylish furniture.*

■ **Claridge (32)** Viale Liegi 62 – 00197 Rome ☎ (06) 8419212 ➥ (06) 8555171 ●●● *An efficient modern hotel with a touch of elegance. The bedrooms are large, well lit and well appointed. The hotel has the latest conference facilities.*

■ **Ritz (33)** Via Chelini 41 – 00197 Rome ☎ (06) 8083751 ➥ (06) 8072916 ●●● *An establishment which comes up to international standards, but with a distinctive Italian flavor. Popular with parties of tourists, particularly Americans and Japanese.*

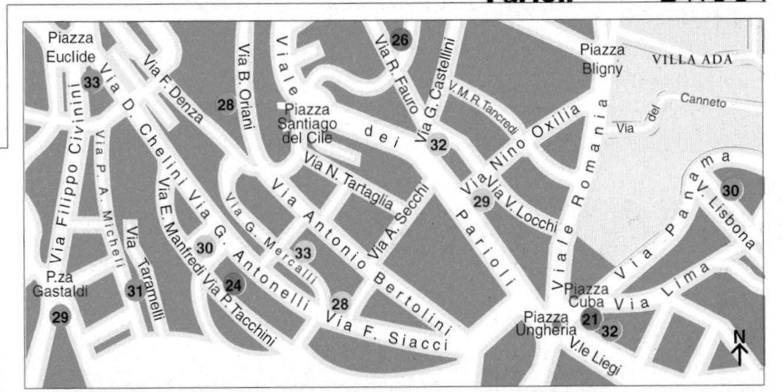
Piazza Euclide
Via D. Chelini
Via F. Denza
Via B. Oriani
Viale dei Parioli
Via R. Fauro
Via G. Castellini
V. M. R. Tancredi
Piazza Bligny
VILLA ADA
Canneto
Via del
Via Filippo Civinini
Via P. A. Micheli
Via Taramelli
Via E. Manfredi
Via G. Antonelli
Via G. Mercalli
Via P. Tacchini
Piazza Santiago del Cile
Via N. Tartaglia
Via Antonio Bertolini
Via A. Secchi
Via Nino Oxilia
Via V. Locchi
Viale Romania
Via Panama
V. Lisbona
Via Lima
Piazza Cuba
Piazza Ungheria
V.le Liegi
Via F. Siacci
P.za Gastaldi
N
26
28
32
29
30
33
31
24
21

28

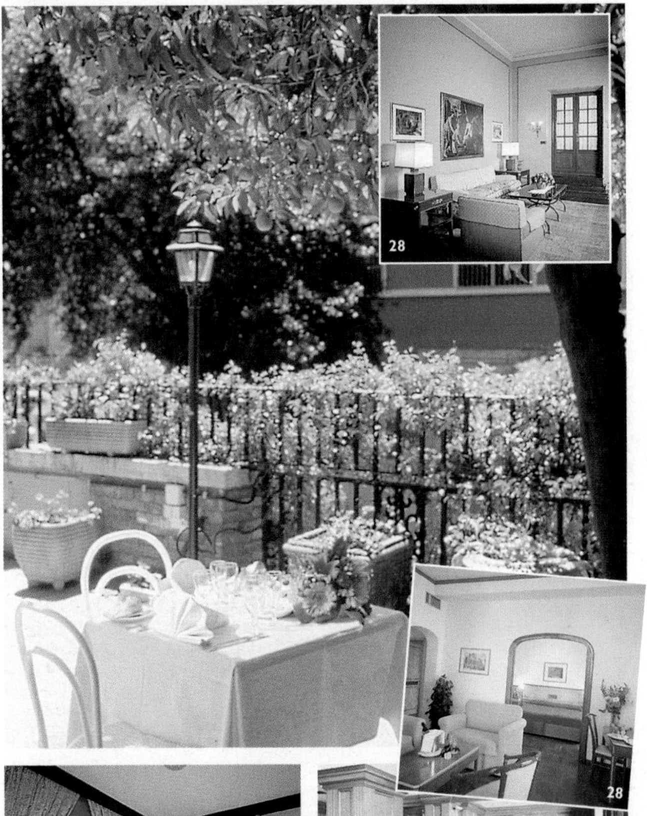

28

28

33

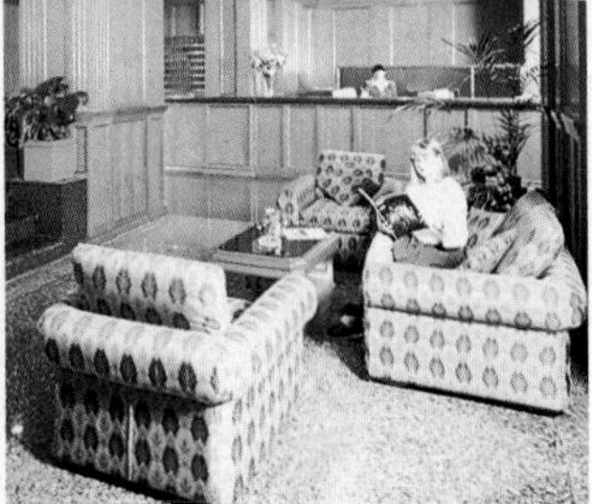

33

Rome is one of the greenest cities in the world. Breaking through the urban fabric here and there, nature finds expression in the highly structured form of the 'Italian garden', and clothes archeological sites and the neighboring parks in a romantic mantle of greenery. The hotels listed below have taken full advantage of these urban oases. Too far out

Where to stay

34

Hotel Cavalieri Hilton (34)
Via Cadlolo 101 – 00136 Rome
☎ (06) 35091 ➟ (06) 35092241

hotel shuttle (Piazza Barberini) ***358 rooms ●●●●●*** *18 suites* *167-878346*

After its latest refurbishment, this must be the most luxurious of Hilton hotels. There is also a breathtaking view of the city spread out below. If that is not enough, it has an outstanding health and fitness center and a park where you can laze by the pool or wander undisturbed in the shade of gigantic umbrella pines and ancient, silvery olive trees.

Sheraton Golf Parco de' Medici (35)
Viale Parco dei Medici 167 – 00148 Rome
☎ (06) 658588 ➟ (06) 6858742

hotel shuttle (Via del Teatro di Marcello) P ***307 rooms ●●●***
15 suites

Conveniently situated on the route from Fiumicino international airport to the EUR ➥ 126, this hotel is not what you expect to find on the outskirts of a big city. It is tucked away in a bend of the Tiber, in a green expanse of meadows and ponds. As well as a swimming pool and tennis courts, it has an eighteen-hole golf course.

of town for first-time visitors to Rome, they are the ideal setting for a longer stay, though not for the budget traveler.

Holiday Inn St. Peter's (36)

Via Aurelia Antica 417 – 00165 Rome ☎ (06) 6642 ➡ (06) 6637190

hotel shuttle (Piazza della Minerva) **P** ***318 rooms ●●●●*** *25,000 lire* *167-7877399*

Not far from St Peter's ➡ 108, the striking feature of this hotel is its sub-tropical atmosphere, enhanced by a riot of luxuriant vegetation and wicker and bamboo furniture. The large bedrooms each have their own sitting room and terrace, more like individual bungalows. ★ It is a real pleasure to explore the surrounding gardens, and to try out the various sports facilities.

Shangri-La Corsetti (37)

Viale Algeria 141 – 00144 Rome ☎ (06) 5916441 ➡ (06) 5413813

M *B EUR Fermi* **P** ***79 rooms ●●*** *17 suites*

This long, low contemporary building blends in with its natural environment, like the many attractive villas in the EUR district ➡ 126. It offers all the comfort and efficiency you would expect of an international hotel, but you could be forgiven for thinking you were in Beverly Hills, especially among the beautiful young people who throng the pool area. The big city seems light years away!

In the area

Hotels and restaurants have always flourished on the approach route to the greatest church in Christendom, catering for the flow of pilgrims to the papal city. ■ Where to eat ➥ 54 ■ Where to eat ➥ 74 ➥ 78 ■ What to see ➥ 108 ■ Where to shop ➥ 150 ➥ 152

Where to stay

Atlante Star (38)

Via Vitelleschi 34 – 00193 Rome
☎ (06) 6873233 ➠ (06) 6872300

23, 64 Via di Porta Castello **60 rooms ●●●** *10 suites* *167-862038* @ *atlante.star@atlantehotels.com*

The reputation of this hotel rests on its panoramic terrace, from which there is an unusual view of the dome of St. Peter's ➥ 108. However, it also offers a high standard of comfort and a wealth of other services. Avoid the rooms overlooking the street, which can be very noisy.

Sant'Anna (39)

Borgo Pio 133 – 00193 Rome
☎ (06) 68801602 ➠ (06) 68308717

23, 492 Via Crescenzio / 64 Borgo Sant'Angelo P **20 rooms ●●** @ *santanna@travel.it*

The Sant'Anna occupies a small 16th-century dwelling in a quiet street, just a short walk from St. Peter's ➥ 108. It is well looked after, from the entrance lobby to the harmoniously decorated bedrooms. Other attractive features are the vaulted breakfast room with its *trompe-l'œil* wall paintings and the pleasant courtyard garden.

Columbus (40)

Via della Conciliazione 33 – 00193 Rome
☎ (06) 6865435 ➠ (06) 6864874

64 Borgo Sant'Angelo P **89 rooms ●●** *3 suites*

Cross the threshold of this venerable establishment and you take a step back in time. With its liveried servants, immense, sumptuously furnished public rooms which still seem to echo with the footsteps of Renaissance princes, frescos ascribed to Pinturicchio and vast courtyard garden, this former monastery exudes a sense of discreet luxury. ★ The dining room, which occupies the former refectory, conveys a hint of monastic austerity.

Cicerone (41)

Via Cicerone 55/c – 00193 Rome
☎ (06) 3576 ➠ (06) 68801383

M *A Lepanto* P **245 rooms ●●●** *5 suites*

This is not the hotel for you if you value local color, the mysterious sense of Rome's three-thousand-year history. However, it does offer the reassuring efficiency, convenience and comfort of a modern international hotel. Not surprisingly it tends to attract primarily a business clientele.

Not forgetting

■ **Olimpic (42)** Via Properzio 2/a - 00193 Rome ☎ (06) 6896650/2 ➠ (06) 68308255 ●● *Comfortable, friendly atmosphere, despite a mixture of styles. Large, cheerful rooms.*

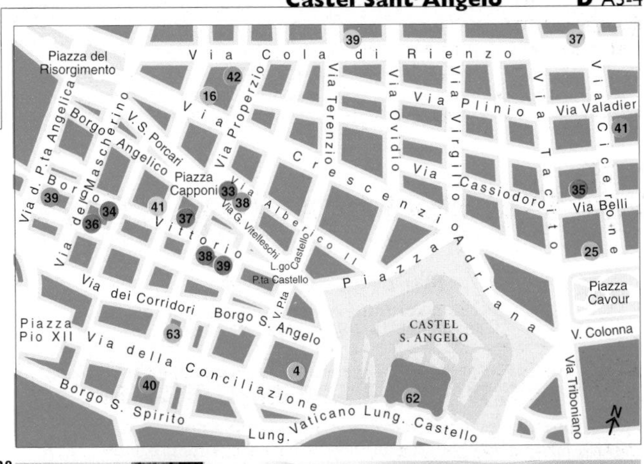
Piazza del Risorgimento
Via Cola di Rienzo
Via Terenzio
Via Ovidio
Via Virgilio
Via Plinio
Via Tacito
Via Valadier
Via Cicerone
Via Properzio
Via Crescenzio
Via Cassiodoro
Via Belli
Piazza Cavour
V. Colonna
Via Triboniano
Piazza Adriana
CASTEL S. ANGELO
Via Alberico II
Via G. Vitelleschi
L.go P.ta Castello
V. P.ta Castello
Piazza Capponi
Borgo Vittorio
Borgo Angelico
V.S. Porcari
Via d. Mascherino
Via d. P.ta Angelica
Via dei Corridori
Borgo S. Angelo
Piazza Pio XII
Via della Conciliazione
Borgo S. Spirito
Lung. Vaticano
Lung. Castello
39
37
42
16
41
35
25
33
38
34
36
63
4
40
62

38

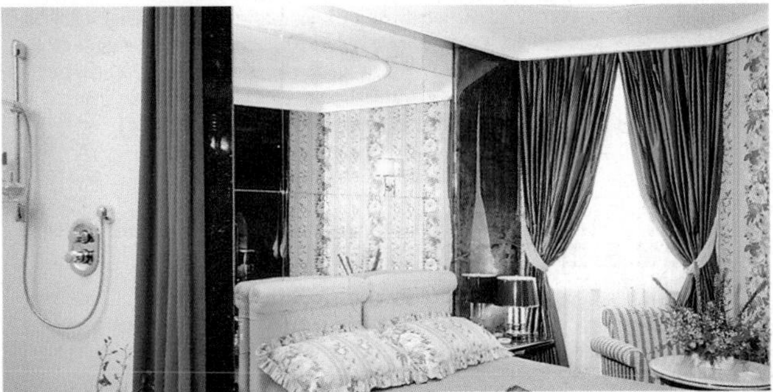

39

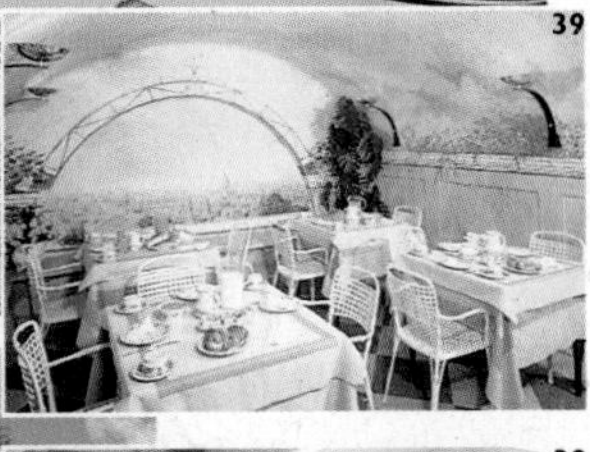

38

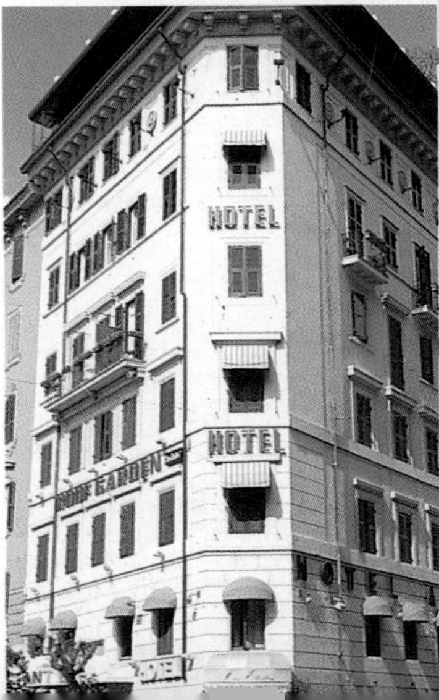

39

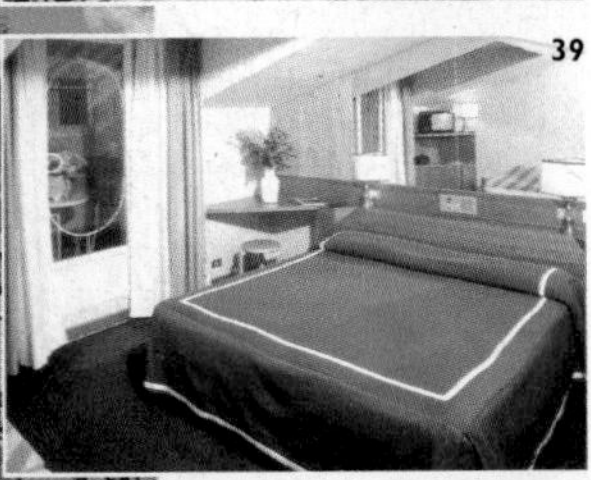

41

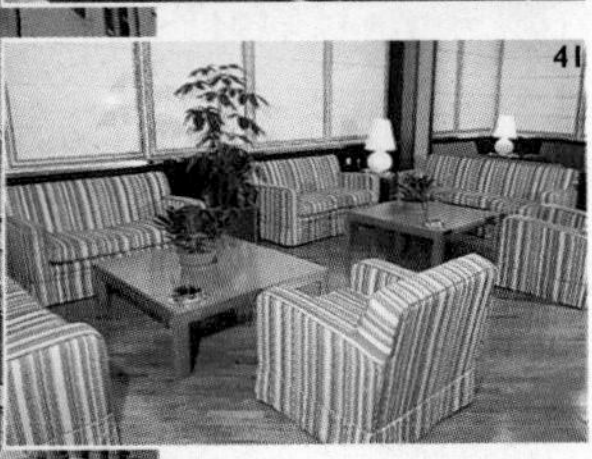

In the area

The intricate network of lanes and squares between Piazza Navona and the Trevi Fountain is an area rich in historic buildings and fine architecture.
■ Where to eat ➡ 56 ■ After dark ➡ 74 ➡ 80 ■ What to see ➡ 114 ➡ 116 ➡ 118 ■ Where to shop ➡ 152 ➡ 154 ➡ 156

Where to stay

Minerva Roma (43)

Piazza della Minerva 69 – 00186 Rome
☎ (06) 69941888 ➡ (06) 6794165

64, 70, 87, 492 Largo di Torre Argentina **P** ***119 rooms*** ●●●● *15 suites* *33,000 lire*

A magnificent 17th-century building restored with a nod to the post-modern age. From lobby to roof-terrace, including furniture and accessories, every aspect has been thoughtfully planned and designed. The highly individual but functional bedrooms are of good size, and many of the pink-marble bathrooms are fitted with hydro-massage baths or showers.

Albergo del Sole al Pantheon (44)

Piazza della Rotonda 63 – 00186 Rome
☎ (06) 6780441 ➡ (06) 69940689

70, 87 Corso del Rinascimento ; 119 Via della Scrofa **P** ***23 rooms*** ●●●● *7 suites*

Opened in 1467, this is undoubtedly the world's oldest hotel. Over the centuries it has accommodated some of Europe's most famous people: Ariosto, Cagliostro, Mascagni, Sartre… Contrasting decorative features include whitewashed walls and frescos, tiled floors and green plants, pillars, cornices and bull's-eye windows opening onto rooms beyond. ★ Opposite the Pantheon ➡ 116, this is the place if you are looking for something quintessentially Italian.

Raphaël (45)

Largo Febo 2 – 00186 Rome ☎ (06) 682831 ➡ (06) 6878993

70, 87, 492 Via Zanardelli ***66 rooms*** ●●●● *6 suites* *14,500 lire*

More than just an elegant hotel with a plush atmosphere and stylish service, this is the sort of place you dream of. The reception area is more like an art gallery, with antique statues and contemporary sculpture on display. Each bedroom, with marble-tiled walls and floor, is decorated differently and furnished with real collectors' items. The hotel is popular with politicians. Bettino Craxi recently used the attic apartment as his base in Rome. From the rooms on the top floor, there are splendid views of the city.

Not forgetting

■ **Fontana (46)** Piazza di Trevi 96 – 00187 Rome ☎ (06) 6786113 / 6791056 ➡ (06) 6790024 ●● *A labyrinthine hotel with a view of the legendary fountain. Even though the sound of falling water and the voices of tourists go on all night, you will hardly regret choosing this hotel.* ■ **Trevi (47)** Vicolo del Babuccio 20/21 – 00187 Rome ☎ (06) 6789563 / 6785894 ➡ (06) 69941407 ●● *A miracle of internal layout, making the best use of the available space in this old building. Small, charming, delightfully furnished and clean.* ■ **Hotel Portoghesi (48)** Via dei Portoghesi 1 – 00186 Rome ☎ (06) 6864231 ➡ (06) 6876976 ● *A private house converted into a hotel, this is an excellent place to stay. The small rooms are all different, cool, quiet and well furnished. Family atmosphere.*

43

45

47

45

The amazing cascade of foliage clothing the façade of the Hotel Raphaël conceals Renaissance decoration carved by Florentine stone-masons.

In the area

In the lively Campo de' Fiori area it is still possible to find simple, comfortable places to stay at affordable prices. Be warned, though: a cheerful, busy street may be unbearable at night. ■ Where to eat ➡ 52 ➡ 58 ➡ 60 ➡ 62 ■ After dark ➡ 80 ➡ 84 ■ What to see ➡ 118

Where to stay

Smeraldo (49)

Vicolo dei Chiodaroli 9 – 00186 Rome
☎ (06) 6875929 / 6892121 ➡ (06) 68805495

44, 170, 710 *Via Arenula* **35 rooms** ● 8, 000 *lire*

This little hotel has become popular following a recent renovation. The public areas and bedrooms, furnished in contemporary style, have all been designed to make the best use of space, with comfort very much in mind.

Rinascimento (50)

Via del Pellegrino 122 – 00186 Rome
☎ (06) 6874813 ➡ (06) 6833518

62, 64 *Corso Vittorio Emanuele II* **19 rooms** ●

This hotel has recently been refurbished. The mixture of styles, from 18th century to Liberty, can be a bit off-putting, but the decent-size rooms are a definite asset.

Teatro di Pompeo (51)

Largo del Pallaro 8 – 00186 Rome
☎ (06) 6872812 / 68300170 ➡ (06) 68805531

62, 64 *Corso Vittorio Emanuele II* **10 rooms** ●● 2 *suites*

This hotel stands in a small square, almost deserted in the evenings, on the site of the ancient Theater of Pompey (55 BC). Vestiges of the classical building are visible in the amazing dining room and basement meeting room. Its small size, the friendliness of the owner, the exposed beams of the attic rooms and terracotta paving all add to the charm.

Arenula (52)

Via di Santa Maria de' Calderari 47 – Rome
☎ (06) 6879454 ➡ (06) 6896188

44, 170, 710 *Via Arenula* **50 rooms** ●

Light, cheerful and cool, harmoniously decorated in white and gray, and spotlessly clean, this hotel offers unfussy comfort and real atmosphere. ★ A place for modern-day exponents of the Grand Tour, eager to be up at dawn and exploring Rome. Book well ahead: the hotel is gaining something of a reputation.

Not forgetting

■ **Albergo della Lunetta (53)** Piazza del Paradiso 68 – 00186 Rome ☎ (06) 6861080/6877630 ➡ (06) 6892028 ● *You can be sure of a courteous welcome. Basic facilities, but has real separate bathrooms. Would suit impecunious art lovers. Some rooms overlook Sant'Andrea della Valle.*

■ **Campo de' Fiori (54)** Via del Biscione 6 – 00186 Rome ☎ (06) 68806865 ➡ (06) 6876003 ● *Small, well-appointed hotel offering a good standard of comfort. Breakfast included, which is rare in this category.*

■ Where to shop ➥ 154 ➥ 158 ➥ 162

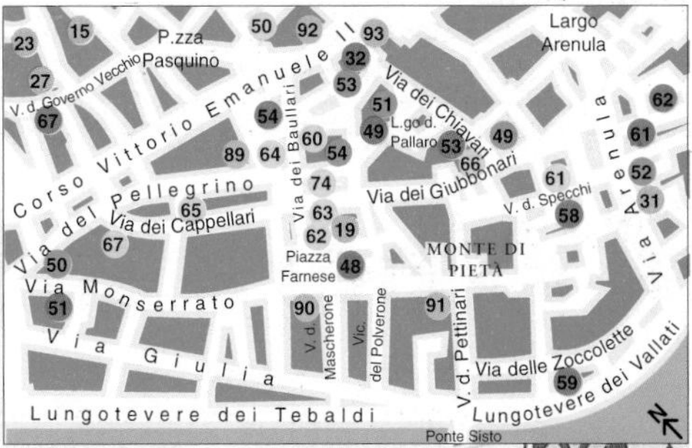
Largo Arenula
P.zza Pasquino
V. d. Governo Vecchio
Corso Vittorio Emanuele II
Via dei Baullari
Via dei Chiavari
L.go d. Pallaro
Via dei Giubbonari
V. d. Specchi
Via Arenula
Via del Pellegrino
Via dei Cappellari
Piazza Farnese
MONTE DI PIETÀ
Via Monserrato
Via Giulia
V. d. Mascherone
Vic. del Polverone
V. d. Pettinari
Via delle Zoccolette
Lungotevere dei Tebaldi
Lungotevere dei Vallati
Ponte Sisto
N
23
15
50
92
93
32
53
27
67
54
51
49
53
66
49
61
62
61
52
31
58
89
64
60
54
74
65
63
62
19
67
50
48
51
90
91
59

50

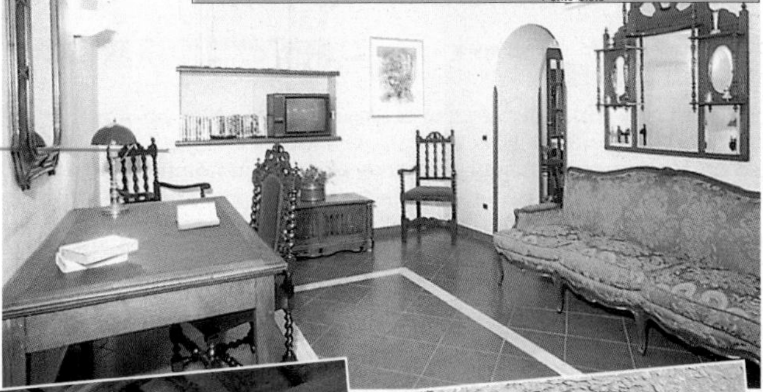

1

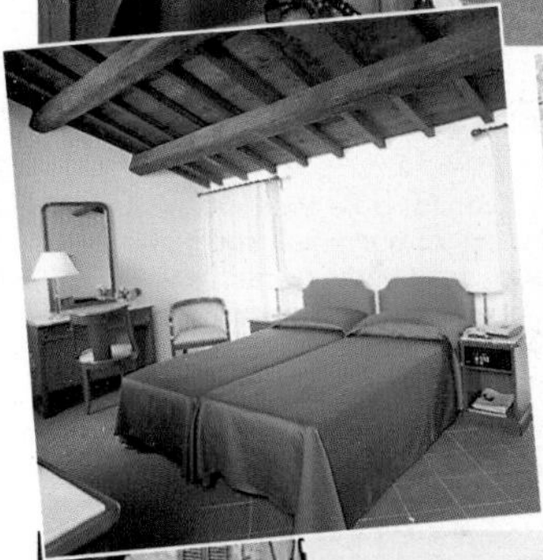

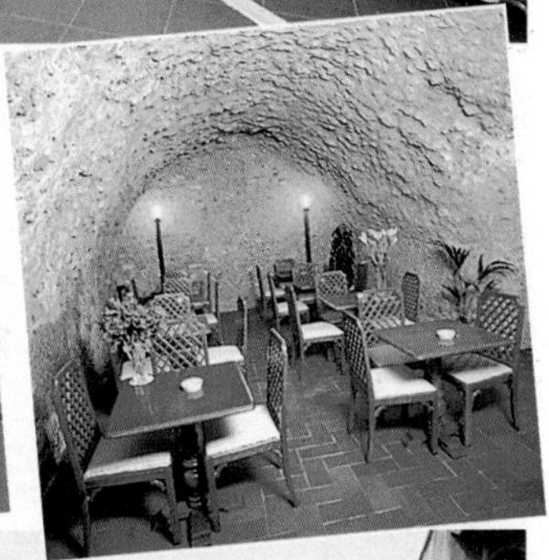

51

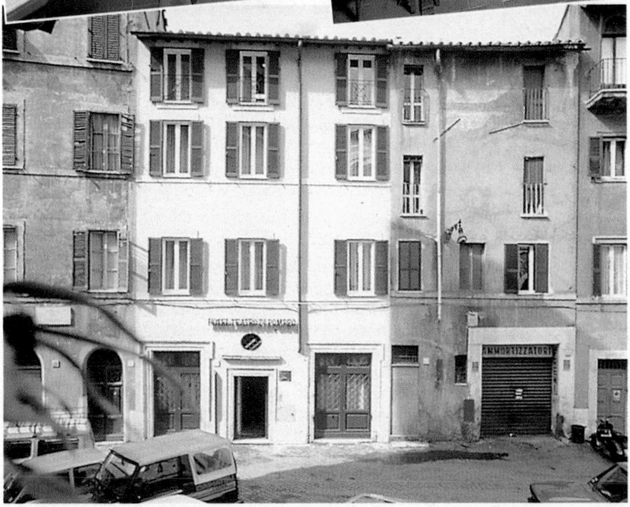
AMMORTIZZATORI

51

In the area

Stay just a stone's throw from the Colosseum and explore Trajan's ancient forum: who could remain unmoved by such a prospect? This district is a place of surprises. Though it attracts many tourists, it has retained its authenticity and old way of life. ■ Where to eat ➡ 62 ■ After dark ➡ 78

Where to stay

Forum (55)

Via Tor de' Conti 25 – 00184 Rome
☎ (06) 6792446 ➠ (06) 6786479

M *B Cavour* *75 rooms* ●●● *5 suites* @ *forum@venere.it*

This former Renaissance *palazzo* is a traditional meeting place of financiers and politicians. Its old-fashioned luxury and the warm glow of its antique furniture create a pleasantly exclusive atmosphere. But its main attraction is the panoramic restaurant on the top floor, which is less prized for its cuisine than for its views of the imperial forums below, particularly impressive at sunset. A pity that the undeniable elegance of the place is spoilt by the unfriendly attitude of the staff.

Richmond (56)

Largo C. Ricci 36 – 00184 Rome
☎ (06) 69941256 ➠ (06) 69941454

M *B Cavour* P *15 rooms* ●● @ *romint@flashnet.it*

A delightful little hotel, well maintained, comfortable and quiet, with staff ready to cater to your every need. The use of warm-colored materials, such as brick and travertine marble, also contributes to the convivial atmosphere. A substantial breakfast is served, in summer, on the roof-top terrace, overlooking the forum. In winter, breakfast is brought to your room. A cozy spot from which to contemplate the decline of empires!

Nerva (57)

Via Tor de' Conti 3 – 00184 Rome
☎ (06) 6781835 / 6793764 ➠ (06) 69922204

M *B Cavour* *18 rooms* ●● *1 suite*

This impeccable little hotel stands opposite Nerva's Forum ➡ 94, at the heart of a district whose working-class way of life will soon be a thing of the past. The Nerva has recently benefited from a complete refurbishment, with liberal use of fine materials, such as walnut, and attractive, colorful wall-hangings. Guests are accommodated in spacious, well-lit bedrooms, some of which are on two levels with exposed beams.

Not forgetting

■ **Bolivar (58)** Via della Cordonata 6 – Rome ☎ (06) 6791614 ➠ (06) 6791025 ●● *A modern, well-appointed hotel tucked away in a small square near Trajan's Forum: a position both quiet and central.*
■ **Grifo (59)** Via del Boschetto 144 – 00184 Rome ☎ (06) 4871395 / 4827596 ➠ (06) 4742323 ● *Clean and unpretentious, comfortable, inexpensive: the kind of address you would pass on to a friend.*
■ **Perugia (60)** Via del Colosseo 7 – 00184 Rome ☎ (06) 6797200 ➠ (06) 6784635 ● *Prices are reasonable, despite the hotel being so close to the Colosseum. Clean and efficient, but you would do well to have breakfast in a local bar.*

■ What to see ➡ 94 ➡ 96 ➡ 100 ■ Where to shop ➡ 140

58

58

55

57

58

The Nerva hotel is named after the emperor who succeeded Domitian in AD 96. In keeping with Nerva's policy of *optimus princeps*, this establishment is attentive to the quality of its service and the well-being of its guests.

In the area

Choose a clear day to go up on the Aventine, one of Rome's seven hills. Falling away to the banks of the Tiber 150 ft below, its public and convent gardens are oases of peace and quiet. However, very few people think of looking for accommodation in this rather secluded district.

Where to stay

Villa San Pio (61)

Via di Sant'Anselmo 19 – 00153 Rome
☎ (06) 5743547 ➟ (06) 5783604

M *B Circo Massimo* P ***65 rooms*** ●●

This hotel gives you the feeling of being an honored guest in an Italian country villa. The busy city could be miles away, especially when you are having breakfast among the statues in the splendid garden, or if you are lucky enough to have reserved one of the bedrooms on the garden side of the hotel. The restful ocher and lilac colors are a perfect foil to the rustic decorative features.

Aventino (62)

Via di San Domenico 10 – 00153 Rome
☎ (06) 5745232 ➟ (06) 5783604

M *B Circo Massimo* ***25 rooms*** ●

The silence of this leafy villa is its greatest asset. Add to this its relaxed family atmosphere and high standard of comfort and you have the perfect retreat from which to explore the art and history of the great city. With its countrified atmosphere, the district is ideal for long walks in the early evening. ★ Undoubtedly one of Rome's best small hotels.

Domus Aventina (63)

Via di Santa Prisca 11/b – 00153 Rome
☎ (06) 57461350 ➟ (06) 57300044

M *B Circo Massimo* P ***26 rooms*** ●●
@ *domus.aventina@italyhotel.com*

This hotel is beside Santa Prisca, the Aventine's oldest place of Christian worship ➡ 98, on one of the tree-shaded streets that climb the hill. Fine mahogany furniture and *trompe-l'œil* decoration lend warmth and color to the public areas. The pleasant bedrooms have stylish furniture and immaculate bathrooms. Some also have a balcony or terrace overlooking the garden, which adjoins the cloister of the church.

Sant'Anselmo (64)

Piazza di Sant'Anselmo 2 – 00153 Rome
☎ (06) 5745174 ➟ (06) 5783604

M *B Circo Massimo* P ***52 rooms*** ●●

A short walk from the Circus Maximus, this hotel is another leafy retreat. Breakfast is served in a garden shaded by orange trees. The marble-paved interior is laid out so that you can read or converse while enjoying the view outside. The well-lit bedrooms are a harmonious mixture of styles, and from the upper floors there are extensive views of the city. Some rooms are specially equipped for disabled people.

What to see ➥ 98

62

64

64

61

'Strascinare'

This verb – literally 'to drag' – indicates a way of lightly frying vegetables boiled with olive oil and garlic (and sometimes other ingredients such as sweet peppers, tomatoes and bacon) to bring out the flavor.

Where to eat

Feeling peckish?

At any time of day you can enjoy a *spuntino* (snack) of the kind sold in *rosticcerie* and *friggitorie*.

Pizza bianca
A 'white pizza', so called, is made without tomatoes. It is a crunchy pizza base served with just oil and salt.

Supplì
The size of a small orange, *supplì are* delicious rice croquettes stuffed with meat and mozzarella cheese and fried in oil.

Italian menus

The menu will probably have five sections. Do as the Romans do! Choose as many dishes as you can eat!

Antipasti A selection of tasty *hors-d'œuvres* (hams, salami, salads, marinated fish, etc.).

Il Primo Pasta is the mainstay of any meal, but *risotto* and *gnocchi* are also included.

Il secondo Meat or fish.

I contorni Side dishes of vegetables are ordered separately.

I dolci Desserts such as tiramisù or pastarella.

Some Roman specialties

Carciofi fritti fried artichokes; ***Filetti di baccalà*** fried cod fillets; ***Fave al guanciale*** broadbeans, onions and ham lightly fried; ***Spaghetti alla carbonara*** a pasta dish with ham, egg and cheese; ***Coda alla vaccinara*** braised oxtail, simmered with wine, tomatoes and sweet peppers; ***Risotto alla romana*** rice, liver, calf's sweetbreads and pecorino cheese.

92 Restaurants

THE INSIDER'S FAVORITES

INDEX BY TYPE

5 PRICE RANGES
- ● less than 50,000 lire
- ● ● 51,000–65,000 lire
- ● ● ● 66,000–80,000 lire
- ● ● ● ● 81,000–100,000 lire
- ● ● ● ● ● more than 100,000 lire

In the area

This district has something of a split personality, torn between the idle luxury of the Via Veneto and the feverish activity of Termini station. Visitors will find a wide range of eating places to choose from, whether their preference is for tradition or novelty, refinement or a tavern-like

Where to eat

Coriolano (1)

Via Ancona 14 – 00198 Rome ☎ (06) 44249863

490, 495 Porta Pia ***Classic cuisine*** ●●●● *Every day noon–3.30pm, 7–11pm*

Elegant surroundings and sophisticated cuisine: the menu includes the very best of Italian gastronomy and traditional Roman fare, prepared with the style one expects of a great restaurant. Seafood of the highest quality: spaghetti with *vongole veraci* (clams harvested in the wild state), *tagliatelle* with lobster. Excellent choice of wines.

Taverna Flavia (2)

Via Flavia 9 – 00187 Rome ☎ (06) 4817787 ➟ (06) 4872028

37, 60, 61, 62 Via XX Settembre ***Classic cuisine*** ●●● *Mon.–Fri. 12.30–3pm, 7.30–11.30pm; Sat. 7.30–11.30pm*

The status of this restaurant as a center of the *dolce vita* is clear from the signed photographs on the walls. However, stardust seems to have contaminated the kitchens, resulting in glamour versions of classic recipes: dishes are served with salmon and caviar garnish, like tinsel on a diva's fur coat!

Trimani Wine Bar (3)

Via Cernaia 37/b – 00185 Rome ☎ (06) 4469630 ➟ (06) 4468351

137, 60, 61, 62 Via Cernaia ***Wine bar*** ● *Mon.–Sat. 11.30am–3pm, 7.30pm–midnight*

Managed by the oldest family of cellarmen in Rome, this wine bar serves some attractive, well-prepared dishes. The choice of food is limited but appetizing, and there is a long list of genuine products from all parts of Italy (meats, cheeses, charcuterie, smoked fish, oysters, etc.). Superb wine list, the result of over a century in the trade.

Cantina Cantarini (4)

Piazza Sallustio 12 – 00187 Rome ☎ (06) 485528

37, 60, 61, 62 Via xx Settembre ***Cuisine from Rome and the Marche region*** ● *Mon.–Sat. 12.30–3.30pm, 7.30–11.30pm*

This *trattoria*, under the management of the Cantarini family for almost a century, successfully combines authenticity and simplicity. The menu includes traditional Roman fare (*carbonara*, *amatriciana*) and dishes from the family's native Marche, such as rabbit *chasseur* and liver with sage. Fish features prominently on Fridays and weekends.

Not forgetting

■ **Costa Balena (5)** Via Messina 5 – 00198 Rome ☎ (06) 8417686 ➟ (06) 44251542 Seafood ●● *The freshest of produce enhanced by the chef's lightness of touch.* ■ **Osteria dell'Arco (6)** Via Pagliari 11 – 00198 Rome ☎ (06) 8548438. Regional cuisine ● *A small restaurant with a friendly country atmosphere. A different region of Italy is featured each week. The concept has caught on: you would be wise to reserve well ahead.*

atmosphere.
■ After dark
➥ 84

2

2

2

3

3

1

The Trimani family have been in the wine trade since 1821. At lunchtime, go for one of the excellent set menus.

In the area

The district near Termini station retains little 19th-century splendor, and now caters mainly for hard-pressed travelers. A few restaurants south of the station are a cut above the rest. ■ Where to stay ➥ 20 ■ After dark ➥ 74 ■ What to see ➥ 102 ■ Where to shop ➥ 140 ➥ 162

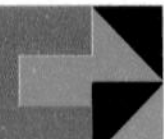

Where to eat

Agata e Romeo (7)

Via Carlo Alberto 45 – 00185 Rome
☎ (06) 4465842 / 4466115 ➡ (06) 4465842

A Vittorio Emanuele ***Creative cuisine*** ●●●● *Mon.–Sat. 1–2.30pm, 8–10.30pm*

A restaurant to change the mind of even the most hardened skeptic when it comes to 'creative cuisine'. The chef's guiding principles are quality and simplicity. Despite his bold approach to combining different ingredients, the familiar flavors persist, and this is the secret of his success. There is an interesting list of regional wines, with some agreeable surprises. Also an excellent set menu, each dish paired with a great wine. Keep some room for a dessert!

Cicilardone a Monte Caruso (8)

Via Farini 12 – 00185 Rome ☎ (06) 483549

A, B Termini ***Cuisine from the Lucca region*** ●●● *Mon. 8pm–midnight; Tues.–Sat. 12 noon–3pm, 8pm–midnight*

Take a virtuoso's knowledge of the traditional cookery of the Basilicata region, season with a pinch of irony from an owner who likes to wait at table, and the result is an agreeable restaurant combining old-fashioned flavors and modern refinement. The *primi piatti* (first courses) are a real delight: the traditional pasta – *orechiette, fusilli, cavatelli* – are all strictly homemade, and the meat dishes, served with light, tasty sauces, are in no way inferior. A good wine list, featuring some excellent wines from the Basilicata region, normally very difficult to find.

Trattoria Monti (9)

Via di San Vito 13/a – 00185 Rome ☎ (06) 4466573

A Vittorio Emanuele ***Cuisine from the Marche region*** ● *Wed.–Mon. 12.30–3.30pm, 7.30–11.30pm*

Elegant, quiet and comfortable, this *trattoria* is the regular *rendezvous* of artists from the nearby Teatro dell'Opera. The traditional cuisine of the Marche region is supplemented with Roman recipes which change with the seasons. There is nevertheless a distinct emphasis on truffles and mushrooms, with a few minor concessions to the current fashion.

Not forgetting

■ **Ristorante del Giglio (10)** Via Torino 137 – 00184 Rome ☎ (06) 4881606 ➡ (06) 48904587 Classic cuisine ●● *Run by a distinguished family of restaurateurs who offer traditional dishes and some interesting inventions inspired by the productions of the Teatro dell'Opera opposite.*

■ **Est Est Est (11)** Via Principe Amedeo 4/a – 00185 Rome ☎ (06) 4741319 Roman cuisine ● *Relaxing, rustic atmosphere and a menu of honest, flavorsome Roman dishes, washed down with the pleasant white wine for which the establishment is named. Excellent pizzas (evenings only).*

■ **Lisa (12)** Via Foscolo 16/18 – 00185 Rome ☎ (06) 70495456 ➡ (06) 8603619 Dishes from Tripoli and Israel ● *The décor is stark in the extreme, but soon forgotten once your palate has been tickled by the exotic flavors on offer. Moderate prices. A few Roman dishes have found their way onto the menu.*

8

7

7

8

8

9

7

The specialties served at the Trattoria Monti hail from the Marche, the region around Ancona on the Adriatic coast of Italy, enriching Rome's own gastronomic tradition.

In the area

The Tridente district, between the Tiber and the Fontana del Tritone, is the daily haunt of foreign visitors, but the local *restaurateurs* seem blissfully unaware of the fact. They continue to spoil their customers as if they were long-established regulars, pandering to their every whim.

Where to eat

Dal Bolognese (13)

Piazza del Popolo 1 – 00187 Rome ☎ (06) 3611426 ➠ (06) 3222799

M *A Flaminio* ***Cuisine from the Emilia-Romagna region*** ●●● *Tues.–Sun. 12.45–3pm, 8.15–11pm*

A setting and décor to overshadow the quality of the cuisine. The food is nevertheless good, in a solid Bolognese tradition, but not too heavy. A haunt of politicians and artists.

Otello alla Concordia (14)

Via della Croce 81 – 00187 Rome ☎ (06) 6791178 ➠ (06) 6791178

M *A Spagna* ***Roman cuisine*** ●● *Mon.–Sat. 12.30–3pm, 7.30–11pm*

In the courtyard of an old Roman residence, this pleasant, relaxed restaurant specializes in the local culinary tradition. Ideal for an evening out with friends, especially if you are a large party. For tables in the courtyard, which becomes a delightful winter garden in the colder months, you would be well advised to book early. Single dishes are a house specialty.

Fiaschetteria Beltramme (15)

Via della Croce 39 – 00187 Rome

M *A Spagna* ***Roman cuisine*** ●● *Mon.–Sat. 12 noon–2.30pm, 7.30–10.30pm*

This tavern, classified as a historic monument, is the place to enjoy traditional Roman family cooking. Mixing with customers of the most varied backgrounds, generations of artists have dined here and decorated the walls with what amounts to a brief history of 20th-century art. No chance of reserving a table: they are not on the telephone!

Del Pollarolo (16)

Via di Ripetta 4/5 – 00186 Rome ☎ / ➠ (06) 3610276

M *A Flaminio* ***Roman cuisine*** ● *Fri.–Wed. 12.30–3pm, 7–11pm*

This small family restaurant has specialized for generations in good, filling food, but also offers gourmet dishes to satisfy even the most demanding gastronome. In the evening, there is a good choice of pizzas, cooked in the all-important wood-fired oven.

Not forgetting

■ **Porto di Ripetta (17)** Via di Ripetta 250 – 00186 Rome ☎ (06) 3612376 ➠ (06) 3227089 Seafood ●●● *First-class fish, cooked with delicacy and inventiveness and served in an elegant setting.* ■ **Osteria Margutta (18)** Via Margutta 82 – 00187 Rome ☎ (06) 3231025 Classic cuisine ●● *Traditional Italian and Roman recipes much appreciated by a regular clientele of celebrities and intellectuals. The décor alone is worth a visit.* ■ **La Penna d'Oca (19)** Via della Penna 53 – 00186 Rome ☎ (06) 3202898 Seafood ●● *All types of fish and some classic dishes for diners who prefer a quiet, intimate setting. In the summer season, reserve a table in the little garden.* ■ **Il Melarancio (20)** Via del Vantaggio 43 – 00186 Rome ☎ (06) 3219382 Classic cuisine ● *Roman and vegetarian food served in an attractive setting, a favorite rendezvous of celebrities.*

■ Where to stay ➥ 24 ■ Where to eat ➥ 52 ■ After dark ➥ 84 ■ What to see ➥ 110 ■ Where to shop ➥ 144 ➥ 146

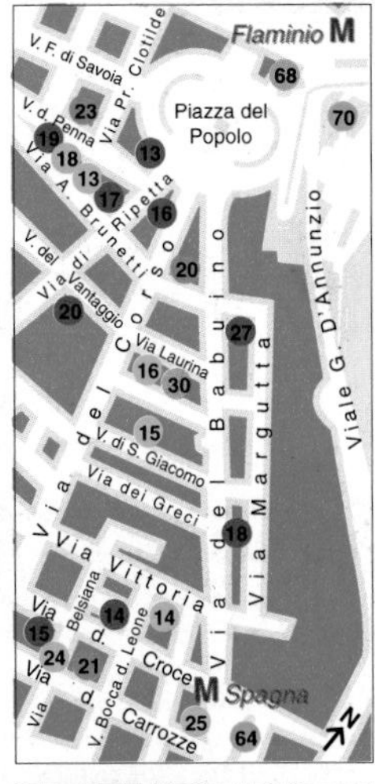

16

15

14

14

15

In the area

Over the years this district's restaurants have had to adapt to a business clientele. Italy's regional cookery has taken an international direction, paying homage to healthy eating and other modern culinary fashions.

■ Where to stay ➡ 28 ■ Where to shop ➡ 148

Where to eat

Al Ceppo (21)

Via Panama 2 – 00198 Rome ☎ (06) 8419696 ➡ (06) 85301370

4, 19 Piazza Ungheria ***Creative cuisine from the Marche region*** ●●● *Tues.–Sun. 12.30–3pm, 7.45–11.15pm*

Two strong-willed sisters, originally from the Marche region, have brought warmth to this elegant restaurant, a popular haunt of professional people. The menu changes at regular intervals, based on slimmed-down versions of native recipes, or using quality ingredients to create new dishes which are never bland or pretentious. In keeping with the restaurant's log symbol, there is a wood fire, and choice cuts of beef and lamb, raised in the pasture lands of the Marche, are cooked on the embers. The wine list is outstanding, featuring some little-known labels that will be all the rage in a few years' time.

Caminetto (22)

Viale dei Parioli 89 – 00197 Rome ☎ (06) 8083946 ➡ (06) 8083291

3, 53, 168 Viale dei Parioli ***Classic cuisine*** ●● *Every day 12.45–3.30pm, 8pm–0.30am*

Elegance and discretion are the hallmarks of this top-quality restaurant, which never disappoints. In recent years, fish have carved out more space on the menu, and the chef has launched into a most agreeable form of creative cooking. In summer, you can lunch or dine outside in a garden overlooking the *boulevard*. Reserve a table to avoid disappointment.

Meeting (23)

Viale Rossini 44 – 00198 Rome ☎ (06) 8551048

4, 19 Piazza Ungheria ***Seafood*** ●● *Mon.–Sat. 12 noon–3pm, 7–11pm*

Rejigged a few years ago to be able to offer a quick lunch to business people, this dignified, elegant restaurant, which makes no concessions to local color or folklore, has become a place to linger. Its cuisine is excellent, light and respectful of its raw materials. The menu changes every day, depending on what fresh, quality products the fish markets have to offer.

Not forgetting

■ **Ambasciata d'Abruzzo (24)** Via Tacchini 26 – 00197 Rome ☎ (06) 8078256 ➡ (06) 8074964 Cuisine from the Abruzzi region ●● *A rustic setting in which to enjoy the flavorsome, filling dishes of the Abruzzi region. Game features prominently in winter.*

■ **Jeff Blynn's (25)** Viale dei Parioli 103/c – 00197 Rome ☎ / ➡ (06) 8070444 American cuisine ●●● *In a delightful, tree-shaded Roman garden, enjoy hamburgers, steaks, French fries and apple pies, just as you would find them in New York. Also serves Italian and international dishes.*

■ **Trattoria Fauro (26)** Via Fauro 44 – 00197 Rome ☎ (06) 8083301 Cuisine from Rome and the Mantua area ● *A friendly local* trattoria *whose menu features both Roman and Mantuan dishes. You would be well advised to reserve a table.*

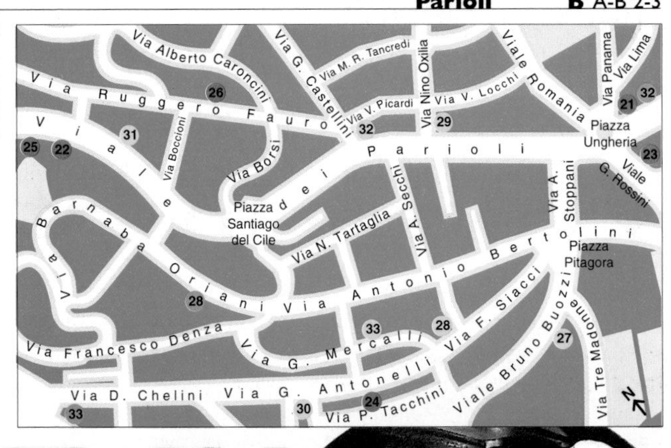
Via Alberto Caroncini
Via G. Castellini
Via M. R. Tancredi
Via Nino Oxilia
Viale Romania
Via Panama
Via Lima
Via Ruggero Fauro
Via V. Picardi
Via V. Locchi
Piazza Ungheria
Viale dei Parioli
Via Boccioni
Via Borsi
Viale G. Rossini
Via A. Stoppani
Piazza Santiago del Cile
Via A. Secchi
Via N. Tartaglia
Via Barnaba Oriani
Via Antonio Bertolini
Piazza Pitagora
Via F. Siacci
Viale Bruno Buozzi
Via Tre Madonne
Via Francesco Denza
Via G. Mercalli
Via G. Antonelli
Via D. Chelini
Via P. Tacchini
N
21
22
23
24
25
26
27
28
29
30
31
32
33

22

22

21

For centuries Rome has been welcoming pilgrims and visitors who, in exchange for its marvels, have good-naturedly accepted anything on offer in the way of food. This is why there are fewer takers than elsewhere for culturally demanding types of cuisine, such as vegetarian cookery. You can count specialized vegetarian restaurants on the fingers of one hand.

Where to eat

27

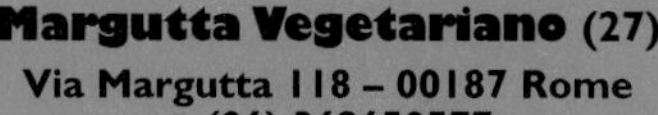

Margutta Vegetariano (27)

Via Margutta 118 – 00187 Rome
☎ (06) 362650577

M *A Flaminio* ●● ▤ ◷ *Every day 10am–2am*

Not so much a restaurant, more a way of life. Spacious, well ventilated, furnished with taste, the Margutta keeps open house for anyone wanting to read, have a cup of tea or chat in the piano bar. The cook makes such imaginative use of the full range of Mediterranean products that you almost forget the rigorous philosophy behind it all. The wines, beers and ciders on offer are all organically produced. An ideal stopping place at any time of day, in the heart of the celebrated Tridente district.

27

Jaya Sai Ma (28)

Via Bargoni 11/18 – 00153 Rome
☎ (06) 3240200

13, 170, 280, 719 Viale di Trastevere ● ◷ *Every day 8pm–midnight*

Of strict vegetarian persuasion, this restaurant also bans alcohol and cigarettes. There is a fixed-price menu with a choice of two pasta dishes and a groaning buffet where you can take your pick of the chef's gastronomic inventions. The quality and variety of the food help you forget the rather chilly modern décor.

27

27

Supernatural (29)

Via del Leoncino 38 – 00186 Rome

M *A Spagna* ***Vegetarian pizzeria*** ● ▤ ◷ *Every day 12.30–3.30pm, 7–11pm*

So 'back to nature' that there is not even a phone! More than fifteen types of vegetable-based pizzas are served in this tiny dining room. The menu is supplemented with generous salads, soybean hamburgers and sausages, pasta dishes and savory tarts, washed down with organically produced draught beer.

However, you will find excellent vegetarian dishes almost everywhere. They are part of the local culinary tradition.

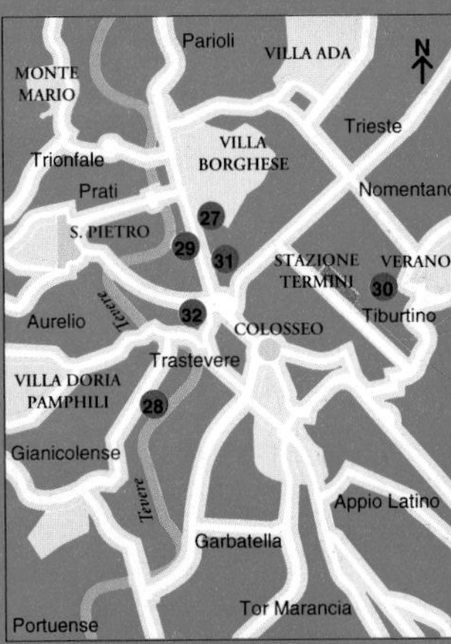

30

Wholesome food for healthy eaters, or for those with a discerning palate in search of new sensations.

28

Arancia Blu (30)

Via dei Latini 65 – 00185 Rome ☎ (06) 4454105

11, 71 Via Tiburtina ; 492 Via dei Ramni ● *Every day 8.30pm–1am*

In the heart of the San Lorenzo district, this light, airy restaurant has an appetizing menu which manages to combine tradition and new thinking. In fact you will hardly mind the absence of meat and fish, and the portions are so generous there is no danger of going home hungry. The interesting wine list is another source of temptation.

Not forgetting

■ **L'Isola (31)** Via della Vite 14 – 00187 Rome ☎ (06) 6792509 ● *Vegetarian club with a rustic, friendly atmosphere. Gourmet menu with regular new additions and a good choice of organically grown wines.* ■ **L'Insalata Ricca (32)** Largo dei Chiavari 85/86 – 00186 Rome ☎ (06) 68803656 Vegetarian and classic cuisine ● *Over twenty kinds of salad and an amazing assortment of pasta dishes. And non-vegetarians need not go without their meat or fish.*

In the area

In the district between St Peter's and the Castel Sant'Angelo, crammed with craftsmen's workshops, time seems to have stood still. The local restaurants aim to match their charming surroundings. ■ Where to stay ➡ 32 ■ After dark ➡ 82 ■ What to see ➡ 108 ■ Where to shop ➡ 152

Where to eat

Les Étoiles (33)

Via Vitelleschi 34 – 00193 Rome
☎ (06) 6873233 ➡ (06) 6872300

23, 64 Via di Porta Castello ***Classic and creative cuisine*** ●●●●● *Every day 12.30–2.30pm, 7.30–10.30pm*

A private elevator whisks you up to a dining room with one of the most amazing views in Rome. From wherever you are sitting, the dome of St Peter's fills the horizon. The décor is stylish and the cuisine, decidedly Mediterranean in inspiration, no less impressive than the view. The menu changes every day, depending on the availability of local produce and the chef's fancy.

33

33

Benito e Gilberto (34)

Via del Falco 19 – 00193 Rome
☎ (06) 68308086 ➡ (06) 6872300

23, 492 Via Crescenzio ***Seafood*** ●●● *Mon.–Sat. 1–3.30pm, 7.30–11pm*

It is immediately obvious that this relaxed family restaurant specializes in the harvest of the sea. The menu is a gastronomic delight: fish, shellfish and crustaceans for appetizers, followed by tempting pasta dishes and some richly garnished main courses. Given the restaurant's popularity and limited capacity, do reserve a table.

Mimì (35)

Via G.G. Belli 59 – 00193 Rome ☎ (06) 3210992

A Lepanto ***Seafood*** ●●● *Mon.–Sat. 1–3.30pm, 7.30–11pm*

Managed by a large family of seafaring people from the island of Ponza, in Campania, this restaurant serves nothing but fish. A good place to experience the honest-to-goodness flavors of traditional Neapolitan cookery.

Arlù (36)

Borgo Pio 135 – 00193 Rome ☎ (06) 6868936

23, 64 Via di Porta Castello ***Creative cuisine*** ●● *Mon.–Sat. 12 noon–3pm, 8–11pm*

Quiet and intimate, elegant and discreet, this restaurant is the perfect setting for a candlelit dinner. The food is sophisticated and imaginative, but does not go beyond the bounds of moderation and good taste.

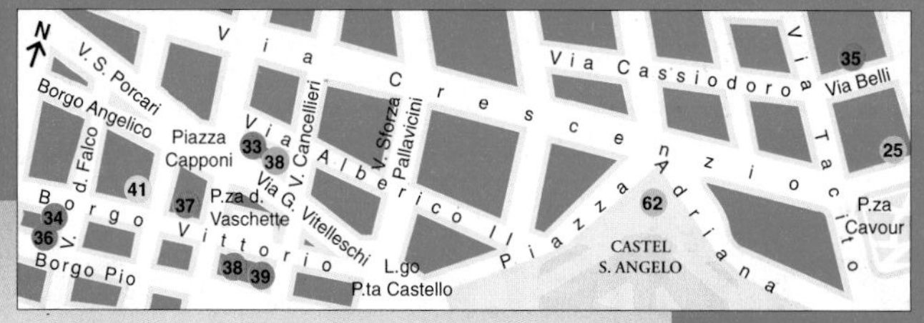

33

36

ARLU A S. PIETRO

RISTORANTE

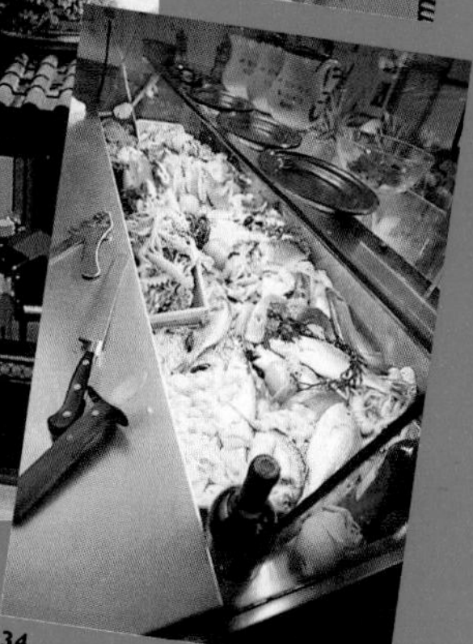

33

34

Not forgetting

■ **Grotte di Castello (37)** Borgo Vittorio 92 – 00193 Rome ☎ (06) 6865143 Regional cuisine ● *A comfortable, quiet restaurant Specialties from Umbria and Campania. Generous size pizzas and a few vegetarian dishes.*

■ **Taverna Angelica (38)** Piazza delle Vaschette 14/a – 00193 Rome ☎ (06) 6874514 Creative cuisine ●● *Dine by candlelight in elegant surroundings.*

■ **Tre Pupazzi (39)** Via dei Tre Pupazzi 1 – 00193 Rome ☎ (06) 6868371 Classic cuisine ● *Almost 400 years old, this tavern serves tasty pasta dishes and pizzas, and some excellent fish.*

In the area

These typically Roman streets, where a nocturnal stroll can be an unforgettable experience, are home to some top-class restaurants whose fame has spread way beyond the confines of Italy. A new generation of aspiring chefs charge more reasonable prices than the established masters.

Where to eat

Papà Giovanni (40)

Via dei Sediari 4 – 00186 Rome ☎ (06) 68804807 ➟ (06) 6865308

70, 87 Corso del Rinascimento ***Roman and creative cuisine*** ●●●●● *Mon.–Sat. 1–3pm, 8–11pm*

This ancient tavern has become a truly elegant venue, without betraying its rustic origins. At first sight, the menu has much in common with those of traditional Roman *trattorie*, but each dish has been given an imaginative new slant and is presented with great artistry. Dishes of Roman inspiration have gradually been supplemented with new inventions, some exciting, others less successful. The wine list is endless, and rather confusing. Reservation recommended.

Il Convivio (41)

Via dell'Orso 44 – 00186 Rome ☎ (06) 6869432

70, 87, 119 Via Zanardelli ***Creative cuisine*** ●●●●● *Mon. 8–11pm; Tues.–Sat. 1–3pm, 8–11pm*

Imagination rules in this tiny restaurant, which has rapidly climbed the heights of culinary fame. The food, which originally seemed designed to provoke, has gradually become more sophisticated and rounded, combining flavors with skill and intelligence: shrimp with sweet peppers, for instance, or pigeon cooked with rosemary and fortified wine. Excellent choice of wines.

La Rosetta (42)

Via della Rosetta 8 – 00187 Rome ☎ (06) 68308841 ➟ (06) 6872852

70, 87 Corso del Rinascimento ; 119 Via della Scrofa ***Seafood*** ●●●●● *Mon.–Fri. 1–3pm, 8–11pm; Sat. 1–3pm*

There is no point discussing skills or technique: in this restaurant they have fish cookery in their blood, and the gift is passed on from father to son. For out-and-out devotees of seafood, prepared to accept the sometimes surprising creations of a chef who nevertheless keeps his imagination under tight control.

Not forgetting

■ **Quinzi e Gabbrielli (43)** Via delle Coppelle 6 – 00186 Rome ☎ (06) 6879389 ➟ (06) 6874940 Seafood ●●●●● *The best fish and the most outrageous prices in the whole of Rome.* ■ **Il Bacaro (44)** Via degli Spagnoli 27 – 00186 Rome ☎ (06) 6864110 Creative cuisine ●● *As packed as a bistro, but the food is sophisticated and imaginative, presented with style and accompanied by excellent wines. You will want to go back.* ■ **Da Gino (45)** Vicolo Rosini 4 – 00186 Rome ☎ (06) 6873434 Roman cuisine ● *A popular trattoria which has preserved its old-fashioned atmosphere, as evidenced by the food and the paintings on the walls. Book ahead.* ■ **Cul de Sac (46)** Piazza di Pasquino 73 – 00186 Rome ☎ (06) 68801094 ➟ (06) 68805092 Wine bar ● *Wine buffs will find an endless list, and dishes specially designed to accompany the best vintages.* ■ **La Campana (47)** Vicolo della Campana 18 – 00186 Rome ☎ (06) 6867820 Roman cuisine ●● *Typically Roman cookery with a touch of class. Comfortable, sheltered surroundings, ideal for talking business.*

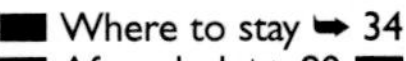

■ Where to stay ➡ 34 ■ After dark ➡ 80 ■ What to see ➡ 116 ■ Where to shop ➡ 152 ➡ 154 ➡ 156

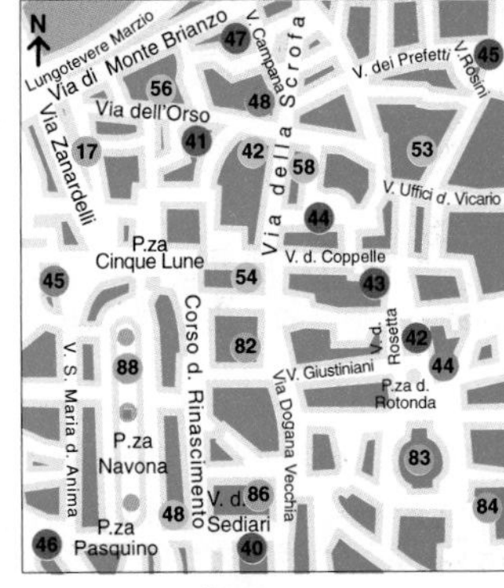

42

Try some delicious fish carpacci in the elegant, dignified setting of La Rosetta.

42

40

41

41

In the area

Within a few yards, you go from an elegant square to a dark alley, from a craftsman's workshop to an arcade crammed with priceless treasures. The same is true of the restaurants: chic venues alternate with lively taverns and candlelit bistros. ■ Where to eat ➥ 62 ■ After dark ➥ 80 ➥ 84

Where to eat

Camponeschi (48)

Piazza Farnese 50 – 00186 Rome ☎ (06) 6874927 ➠ (06) 6865344

62, 64 Corso Vittorio Emanuele II ***Classic and seafood cuisine*** ●●● *Mon.–Sat. 7.30pm–0.30am*

An elegant restaurant providing good service, the Camponeschi caters for celebrities attracted by a varied menu combining highly creative fish specialties with traditional Roman fare and some of the great international classics (*soufflés*, game in season). The cellar is equally impressive. Several charming little rooms are available for customers wanting to dine in private.

Dar pallaro (49)

Largo del Pallaro 15 – 00186 Rome ☎ (06) 68801488

62, 64 Corso Vittorio Emanuele II ; 70, 87 Corso del Rinascimento ***Roman cuisine*** ● *Tues.–Sun. 12.30–3.30pm, 7.30pm–0.30am*

An endless procession of Roman dishes served until late at night in a family-run restaurant with real country roots. *Fagioli al fiasco* (haricot beans cooked in a flask with herbs) and homemade *rigatoni* will appeal to lovers of strong, earthy flavors. In summer you can dine on the terrace without finding the district's noisy bustle too intrusive.

Il Cardinale (50)

Via delle Carceri 6 – 00186 Rome ☎ / ➠ (06) 6869336

62, 64 Corso Vittorio Emanuele II ***Roman cuisine*** ●● *Mon.–Sat. 12.30–3pm, 8–11.30pm*

Privacy, elegance and a sense of proportion rule in this little restaurant, where the daily menu depends on what products are available on the local market. Quality ingredients form the basis of every dish, which does not preclude inventiveness on the part of the chef. Try his soups or the flavorsome *zucchini alla velletrana*. First-class wine list.

Not forgetting

■ **Pierluigi (51)** Piazza de' Ricci 144 – 00186 Rome ☎ (06) 6861302 ➠ (06) 68807879 Classic cuisine ●● *A restaurant disguised as a small Roman trattoria, friendly and relaxed, with tables set in a quiet little square.*
■ **Il Drappo (52)** Vicolo del Malpasso 9 – 00186 Rome ☎ (06) 6877365 Sardinian cuisine ●● *Sardinian cookery served with sophistication in an attractive, intimate setting, ideal for a confidential conversation. Be sure to reserve a table.*
■ **Arnaldo ai Satiri (53)** Via di Grottapinta 8 – 00186 Rome ☎ (06) 6861915 Classic cuisine ● *Everything, from the highly individual décor to the unusual dishes on offer, expresses the personality of this restaurant's owners. You will either love it or hate it.* ■ **Ditirambo (54)** Piazza della Cancelleria 74 – 00186 Rome ☎ (06) 6871626 Classic cuisine ● *A menu that includes both unusual and classic dishes, drawing on the best in Italy's regional traditions.*
■ **Hostaria dei Banchi Vecchi (55)** Via dei Banchi Vecchi 129 – 00186 Rome ☎ / ➠ (06) 6832310 Classic cuisine ● *Halfway between a tavern and a restaurant, this establishment is justly proud of its magnificent pasta dishes and risottos, which change from day to day, and its tempting range of homemade desserts. Wood-fired oven for making pizzas and focaccia.*

■ What to see ➥ 118
■ Where to shop
➥ 154 ➥ 158 ➥ 162

48

49

49

48

50

50

In the area

With a history dating back four hundred years, Rome's Jewish district ➡ 120 has preserved its atmosphere and traditions. The restaurants perpetuate some of the old ways, with Jewish dishes included on their menus alongside gentile cuisine. ■ Where to stay ➡ 36 ■ After dark ➡ 84

Where to eat

Piperno (56)

Via Monte dei Cenci 9 – 00186 Rome
☎ (06) 68806629 ➡ (06) 50915487

44, 170, 710 Via Arenula ***Roman Jewish cuisine*** ●●● *Tues.–Sat. 12.15–2.30pm, 8–10.30pm; Sun. 12.15–2.30pm*

This temple of Roman Jewish cookery seems to belong to another age: severe, outmoded décor and rather conservative food. But the chef is a real artist, respecting the traditional flavors but with a certain lightness of touch. His *carciofi alla giudia* (small crispy fried artichokes) are out of this world.

Giggetto (57)

Via del Portico d'Ottavia 21/a – 00186 Rome
☎ (06) 6861105 ➡ (06) 6832106

44, 170, 710 Via Arenula ***Roman cuisine*** ●● *Tues.–Sun. 12.30–3pm, 7.30–11pm*

Right in the heart of the ghetto, this classic Roman restaurant is out of temptation's way where new-fangled ideas are concerned. Jewish dishes, such as *carciofi alla giudia* or fillets of *baccalà* (cod), are the star turns. Ideal for a relaxed evening with friends.

Osteria degli Specchi (58)

Via degli Specchi 5 – 00179 Rome ☎ (06) 6861566

44, 170, 710 Via Arenula ***Classic cuisine*** ●● *Mon.–Sat. 8pm–2.30am*

Tavern downstairs, serving meat and pasta dishes at modest prices; restaurant upstairs, offering a more sophisticated form of seafood cookery. What they both share is careful preparation and a lightness of touch, and they owe much to regional styles of cookery. The tasteful setting attracts well-known figures from the world of entertainment..

Evangelista (59)

Via delle Zoccolette 11/a – 00185 Rome ☎ (06) 6875810

44, 170, 710 Via Arenula ***Roman cuisine*** ●● *Mon.–Sat. 8–11.30pm*

The chef's *carciofo al mattone* (artichoke 'brick') is not to be missed. The menu features an irresistible abundance of gourmet Roman dishes, with a few borrowings from northern and southern Italy. The décor is unpretentious, the atmosphere relaxing.

Not forgetting

■ **Vecchia Roma (60)** Piazza di Campitelli 18 – 00186 Rome ☎ / ➡ (06) 6864604 Classic cuisine ●●● *Good solid cooking in a charming corner of the capital.* ■ **Bottega del Vino da Bleve (61)** Via di Santa Maria del Pianto 9/a – 00186 Rome ☎ / ➡ (06) 6865970 Wine bar ● *A good place for a quick lunch. Appetizing dishes and excellent wines to match, served by the glass.* ■ **Zi Fenizia (62)** Via di Santa Maria del Pianto 64/65 – 00186 Rome ☎ (06) 6896976 Kosher pizzeria ● *Slices of pizza, all strictly kosher, and the chance to try some really original dishes.*

What to see ➥ 120
Where to shop ➥ 158

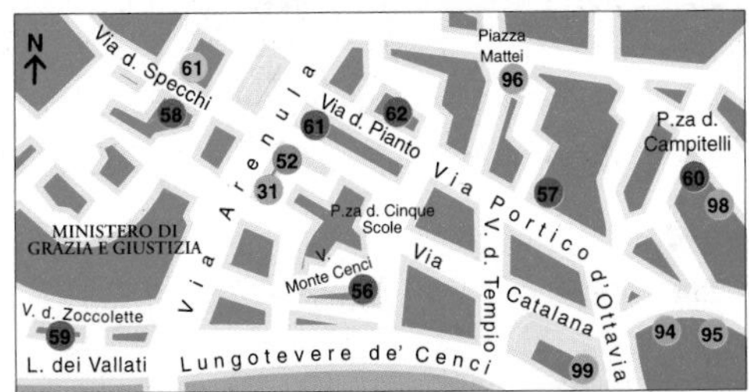

56

56

57

57

59

57

There is an old idea that a Roman *osteria* is a tavern where you can have an enjoyable meal, washed down with quantities of wine, for a very small outlay. This kind of establishment is on the way out, or rather it is being replaced by a growing number of wine bars. They continue the tradition of serving appetizing food at affordable prices to accompany their wines.

Where to eat

Osteria dell'Angelo (63)
Via Bettolo 24 – 00195 Rome ☎ (06) 3729470

M *A Ottaviano* **Roman cuisine** ● *Mon.–Fri. 12.30–2.30pm, 8–10.30pm; Sat. 8–10.30pm*

You eat for a fixed price in this typical *osteria*, which since 1989 has been run by a former rugby player. Enjoy the authentic Roman flavors of wild-boar sausage, *rigatoni alla pajata* (pasta with tripe), *minestra di arzilla* (skate soup) or *coda alla vaccinara* (oxtail in a white-wine and tomato sauce). *À la carte* at lunchtime, ★ 30,000-lire menu in the evening, wine included. The place is extremely popular, so book several days ahead.

Cavour 313 (64)
Via Cavour 313 – 00184 Rome ☎ / ➟ (06) 6785496

M *B Cavour* **Wine bar** ● *Mon.–Sat. 12.30–2.30pm, 7.30pm– 0.30am*

It was the Cavour's (once) young owners who first had the idea of serving a range of tasty snacks to accompany a wide choice of good wines, served by the glass. The fashion for wine bars has since caught on worldwide. The ritual is repeated every evening. The quality is as good as ever and the prices still very reasonable.

66

63

At the Osteria dell'Angelo, enjoy all the specialties of traditional Roman cookery in a delightful setting.

63

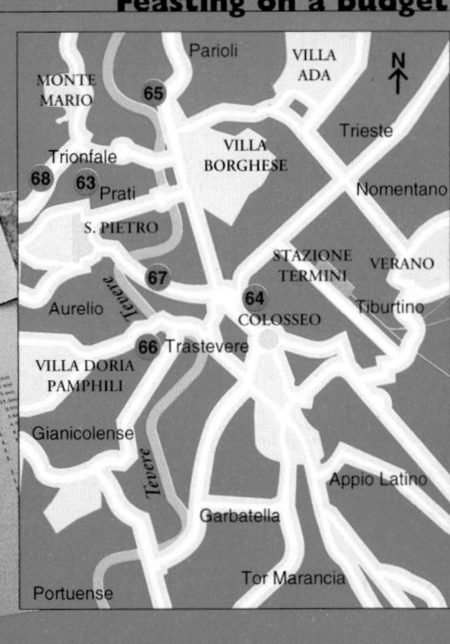

63

Il Tiepolo Bistrot – Bottiglieria (65)

Via Tiepolo 3 – 00196 Rome ☎ (06) 3227449

225 Via Flaminia **Classic cuisine** ● *Mon.–Sat. noon–3.30pm, 7.30pm–midnight*

A former wine-and-oil shop saved by an enterprising young couple. They serve a limited number of straightforward dishes (salads, soups, cheese and charcuterie, stuffed baked potatoes) and some good wines. The *bistro*-style tables are always crowded. Popular with show-biz types.

Kottabos – Il Gioco del Vino (66)

Via dei Fienaroli 30/a – 00153 Rome ☎ (06) 5897196

44, 75, 170 Viale di Trastevere **Wine bar** ● *Mon.–Sat. 8pm–1am*

Some thoroughbred vintages – some famous, others little known – are served with this wine bar's interesting range of food. There are some beautifully cooked dishes, as well as excellent charcuterie and cheeses from all parts of Italy. For amateur wine buffs, there is the additional pleasure of discovering the great wines of tomorrow.

Not forgetting

■ **Da Baffetto (67)** Via del Governo Vecchio 11 – 00186 Rome ☎ (06) 6861617 Pizzeria ● *This tried-and-tested pizzeria is crowded every evening with locals and tourists. Variety, quality and modest prices make it worth the long wait for a table.* ■ **Sagra del Vino da Candido (68)** Via Marziale 5 – 00136 Rome ☎ (06) 39737015 Roman cuisine ● *A trattoria of the old school, which will appeal to lovers of strong flavors, a relaxed setting and the smooth Olevano wine.*

66 64

In the area

In this district a number of good restaurants stand out like beacons in the night. Why not use them as starting points for discovering a part of Rome with a contradictory personality, which is not usually included in tourist itineraries?

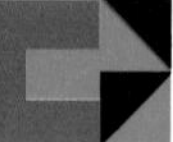

Where to eat

Sora Lella (69)

Via di Ponte Quattro Capi 16 – 00186 Rome ☎ / ➠ (06) 6861601

23, 717, 780 Lungotevere de' Cenci ***Roman cuisine*** ●●● *Mon.–Sat. 12.50–2.30pm, 7.50–10.50pm*

It was here, on an island in the Tiber (the Isola Tiberina), that the sister of actor Aldo Fabrizi established her culinary kingdom. An actress herself, Sora Lella performed as brilliantly in her restaurant as she did on stage. Her son has since taken over and continues the tradition, adding his own touch of grace and warmth. The emphasis is Roman, but the restaurant also serves Jewish dishes, and some rarities only to be found in the pages of turn-of-the-century cook books.

Peccati di Gola (70)

Piazza dei Ponziani 7/a – 00153 Rome
☎ (06) 5814529 ➠ (06) 5816840

23, 717, 780 Lungotevere degli Anguillara ***Seafood*** ●●● *Tues.–Sun. 1–3pm, 8pm–midnight*

'The sins of gluttony': a name well chosen in the light of this restaurant's choice of fish dishes, prepared in classical style with the odd excursion into creative cuisine and strongly flavored Calabrian cookery. There are several well-balanced fixed-price menus. The setting is elegant but restful. In summer you would do well to reserve a table, especially if you prefer to eat outside.

Hostaria del Campidoglio (71)

Via dei Fienili 56 – 00186 Rome ☎ (06) 6780250

23, 717, 780 Lungotevere Pierleoni ***Cuisine of the Lucania region*** ●● *Mon.–Sat. 12.30–3pm, 7.30–11.30pm*

This restaurant enjoys an extraordinary position between the Capitoline Hill ➥ 92 and the Tarpeian Rock. Its food is no less outstanding, based on a range of succulent dishes from the Basilicata region, which are difficult to find outside their region of origin. The body and nose of a good bottle of Aglianico from the same region will considerably enhance your enjoyment, making the meal an unforgettable experience.

Not forgetting

■ **Panattoni (72)** Viale di Trastevere 53 – 00153 Rome ☎ (06) 5800919
Pizzeria ● *A pizzeria serving the full range of pizza specialties, well cooked and served with speed and courtesy to a clientele of locals and tourists from all parts of the world.*

■ **Papa Re (73)** Via della Lungaretta 149 – 00153 Rome ☎ (06) 58142069
Seafood ● *Installed in an old tavern, a small restaurant serving honest Roman fare and some appetizing fish dishes. Reserve a table.*

■ **Fidelio Vini (74)** Via degli Stefaneschi 5/7 – 00153 Rome
☎ (06) 5803041 Roman cuisine ● *All the atmosphere of an old Roman tavern. Excellent choice of wines to go with savory tarts,* bruschetta *(toasted bread with oil and garlic), salads, charcuterie, cheeses and desserts.*

What to see ➥ 98 ➥ 106 ➥ 120 Where to shop ➥ 160

71

69

Pasta e ceci (pasta and lentils) and *abbacchio brodettato* (lamb in broth) are two of the traditional dishes serves at Sora Lella.

69

70

70

70

In the area

Trastevere is a little paradise, but full of pitfalls for the unsuspecting. For shopping and atmosphere it is a wonderful place, but do not trust to luck when it comes to eating out. Do your research, however, and you may be agreeably surprised.

Where to eat

Alberto Ciarla (75)

Piazza di San Cosimato 40 – 00153 Rome
☎ (06) 5818668 ➟ (06) 5884377

44, 75, 170 Viale di Trastevere ***Seafood*** ●●●● *Mon.–Sat. 8.30pm–0.30am*

With the change in generations, this old *trattoria* has become a high place of seafood cookery. Elegant setting, sophisticated clientele, and an unusual mixture of creative cuisine, classic recipes and genuine Mediterranean fare. It all revolves around the exuberant personality of Alberto Ciarla, a former harpoon fisherman, who is capable of brave, unconventional experiments, but quite incapable of serving any fish which is not absolutely fresh. His raw-fish dishes are superb. Excellent wine list. You would be wise to book ahead.

Da Paris (76)

Piazza di San Calisto 7/a – 00153 Rome ☎ (06) 5815378

44, 75, 170 Viale di Trastevere ***Roman cuisine*** ●●● *Tues.–Sat. noon–3pm, 7.30–11pm; Sun. noon–3pm*

It must be difficult to set up in the heart of Trastevere, hang out the tired old 'Roman cooking' sign, and emerge as something special. But this restaurant is managed with such elegance and sophistication that you soon forget the noisy, folkloristic image of Rome's most picturesque district. The dishes are traditional (skate soup, oxtail, etc.), but interpreted with a style that brings out the most delicate nuances. They serve a delicious *fritto misto* of vegetables. First-class cellar.

Antica Pesa (77)

Via Garibaldi 18 – 00153 Rome ☎ (06) 58331518 ➟ (06) 5809236

44, 75, 170 Viale di Trastevere ; 23, 65, 280 Lungotevere Sanzio ***Classical cuisine*** ●●● *Mon.–Sat. noon–3.30pm, 7.30–11pm*

This restaurant is housed in a 17th-century convent, with a spectacular indoor garden. The style of cuisine would appeal to grandmother's generation. The dishes are traditional, but elegant and well balanced. According to old custom, a different dish is featured each day: *gnocchi* on Thursday, fish soup on Friday, etc.

Not forgetting

■ **Checco er Carrettiere (78)** Via Benedetta 10 – 00153 Rome ☎ (06) 5800985 ➟ (06) 5884282 Roman cuisine ●●●● *For forty years, this monument to traditional cookery has victoriously resisted the forces of change, becoming a living legend in the process.* ■ **Dieci Pasta e Ceci (79)** Vicolo della Scala 3 – 00153 Rome ☎ (06) 5897097 Roman cuisine ● *A family-run trattoria with a relaxed, friendly atmosphere, serving genuine local food.*
■ **Fantasie di Trastevere (80)** Via di Santa Dorotea 6 – 00153 Rome ☎ (06) 5881671 ➟ (06) 5817343 Classic cuisine ●●●● *A charming, historic venue, where you can enjoy traditional Neapolitan/Roman entertainment while you eat. Worth a visit, despite the prices.*

What to see ➥ 106
Where to shop ➥ 160

77

77

77

76

75

In a setting worthy of Jules Verne, Alberto Ciarla serves a version of ***pasta e fagioli*** (pasta and dwarf beans) enriched with seafood.

75

75

In the area

The triangle formed by Piazza Vittorio, San Giovanni in Laterano and the Colosseum is an eldorado for gourmets. There is an abundance of historical buildings, but tourists often eat elsewhere, leaving local chefs to take their time over the saucepans. ■ What to see ➥ 100 ➥ 104

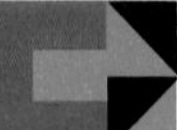

Where to eat

Ai 3 Scalini da Rosanna e Matteo (81)

Via Santi Quattro 30 – 00184 Rome ☎ (06) 7096309 ➠ (06) 7002835

85 Via di San Giovanni in Laterano **Classic cuisine** ●●●
Tues.–Sun. noon–3pm, 7pm–midnight

A place of elegance and sophistication with two small dining rooms serving two quite different, though complementary, menus: on one hand, a modern version of traditional Roman cuisine with the rough edges taken off; on the other, some of the great Italian and international dishes (excellent game in season), treated with flair and imagination. The restaurant is small and the service very personal, so you are strongly advised to book ahead.

Charly's Saucière (82)

Via di San Giovanni in Laterano 270 – 00184 Rome ☎ (06) 70495666 ➠ (06) 70494700

85 Via di San Giovanni in Laterano **Franco-Swiss cuisine** ●●●
Tues.–Fri. 1–3pm, 8pm–midnight; Sat., Mon. 8pm–midnight

This pleasant, discreetly elegant venue is the best of Rome's very few French restaurants. The menu also includes some Swiss dishes – tasty *roesti* and real fondues – and some of the classics of international cuisine, prepared with professionalism and talent. Top-quality cuts of meat, airy soufflés and delicious pâtés, strangely out of place in the eternal city. The wine list naturally emphasizes French wines, of which there is a good choice. Excellent desserts.

Cannavota (83)

Piazza di San Giovanni in Laterano 20 – 00184 Rome ☎ (06) 77205007

16, 85, 715 Via Merulana **Roman cuisine** ●● *Thurs.–Tues. 12.30–3pm, 7.30–11pm*

This is the very model of a Roman *trattoria*: friendly, cheerful and relaxed. They serve many traditional Roman dishes, some in their own incomparable house style. There is an interesting selection of pasta and risotto dishes based on seafood. Extremely popular, so book ahead to be sure of a table.

Not forgetting

■ **Isidoro (84)** Via Ostilia 23 – 00184 Rome ☎ (06) 7008266 Classic cuisine ● *A typical local* trattoria *which has made its name with some extraordinary pasta and risotto dishes. You will not get a table unless you book.*

■ **Buoni Amici (85)** Via Aleardi 4 – 00185 Rome ☎ (06) 70491993 Classic cuisine ● *Quality food, often inspired by the cooking of the Puglie region, birthplace of the present owners. Both meat and fish dishes gain from the beautifully prepared vegetables.*

■ **Il Tempio di Iside (86)** Via Verri 4 – 00184 Rome ☎ (06) 7004741 Classic cuisine and seafood ●● *Fish, expertly prepared, holds pride of place here, but there are also some good meat dishes of Sardinian inspiration.*

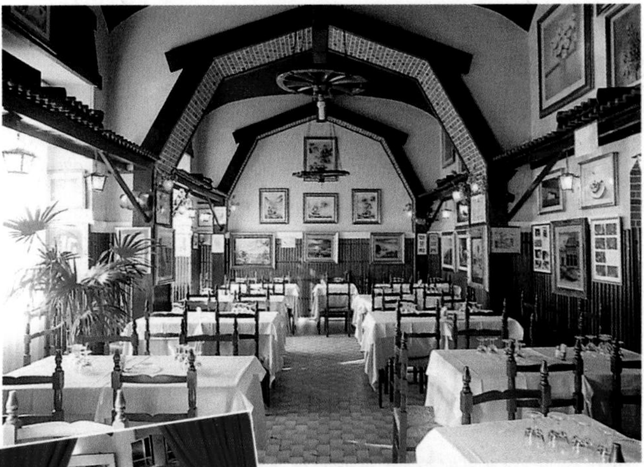

83

82

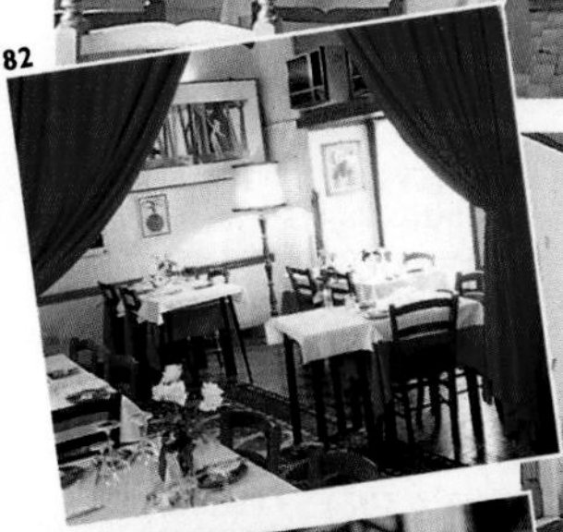

81

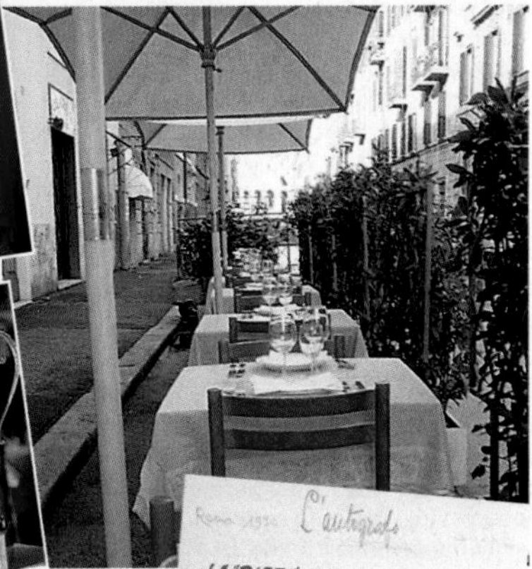

83

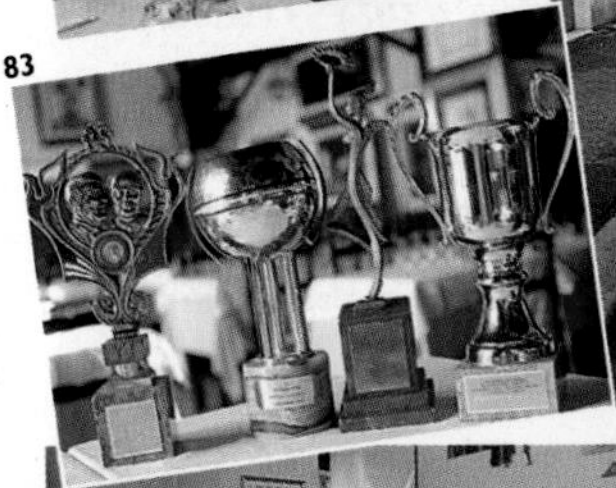

83

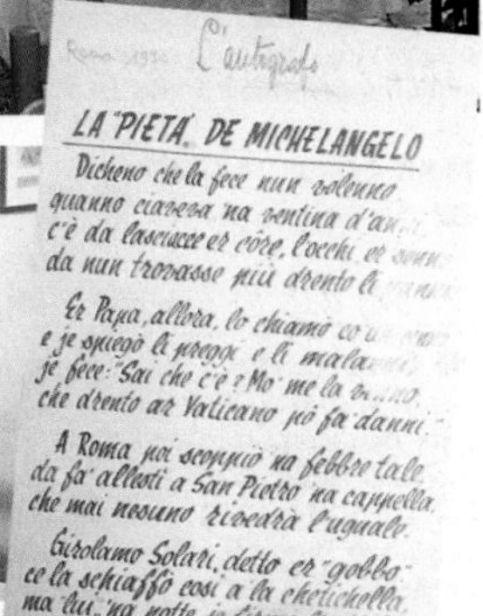

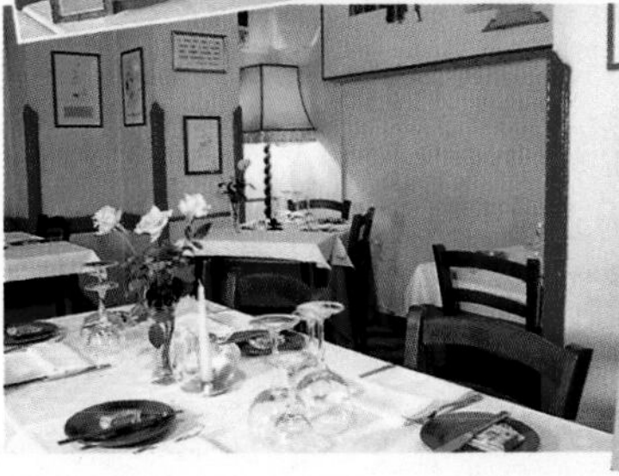

L'autografo

LA "PIETÀ" DE MICHELANGELO

Dicheno che la fece nun volenno
quanno ciaveva 'na ventina d'an
c'è da lasciacce er còre, l'occhi er
da nun trovasse più drento li

Er Papa, allora, lo chiamò co
e je spiegò li preggi e li mala
je fece: "Sai che c'è? Mo' me la
che drento ar Vaticano pò fa' danni."

A Roma poi scoppiò 'na febbre tale
da fa' allesti a San Pietro 'na cappella
che mai nessuno rivedrà l'uguale.

Girolamo Solari, detto er "gobbo"
ce la schiaffò così a la chetichella,
ma lui.. 'na notte je firmò, l'addobbo!

82

In the area

Many dishes based on offal were developed here in the old slaughterhouse district. Try such specialties as *coda alla vaccinara* (oxtail) or *rigatoni con la pajata* (pasta with tripe) – born of poverty maybe, but sublime. The Testaccio still maintains the traditions of working-class gastronomy. A

Where to eat

Checchino dal 1887 (87)

Via di Monte Testaccio 30 – 00153 Rome ☎ / ➟ (06) 5743816

M *B Piramide* **Roman cuisine** ●●● *Tues.–Sat. 12.30–3pm, 8–11pm; Sun. 12.30–3pm*

With over a century of experience, this family approaches Roman cuisine with an almost archeological care and rigor. For their traditional recipes, they use only the choicest ingredients and have made a study of ancient cooking techniques. The dishes may have the same names as those served in other restaurants, but the effect is somehow different. The food is served with a wonderful choice of older and newer wines, selected with just one criterion in mind: quality. Pay a visit to the extraordinary cellar dug into the *monte dei cocci*, the centuries-old accumulation of Roman amphora crocks which forms the Monte Testaccio.

Perilli (88)

Via Marmorata 39 – 00153 Rome ☎ (06) 5742415

M *B Piramide* **Roman cuisine** ●● *Thurs.–Tues. 12.30–2.30pm, 8.30–10.00pm*

Never mind the confusion, the hubbub of conversation, nor the comings and goings of waiters more concerned with their own exchanges than with the packed mass of customers. Here, every evening, you will find a perfect sample of traditional Roman cuisine: tripe and tomato, lamb's offal with artichokes, artichokes *alla romana*... Better to leave your prejudices and the fear of strong rustic flavors in the cloakroom. Wine is served by the *carafe*, but this need not stop you ordering a bottle or two. This ritual has been going strong for over a century, and is still as popular as ever.

Da Felice (89)

Via Mastro Giorgio 29 – 00153 Rome ☎ (06) 5746800

M *B Piramide* **Roman cuisine** ● *Mon.–Sat. 12.30–2.30pm, 8.30–10pm*

A classic *trattoria*, extremely popular with big eaters and celebrities looking for an anonymous, relaxing setting designed for a quiet dinner with friends. The full-flavored local dishes are set off by cool wines from the Castelli Romani. The owners have been remarkably faithful in preserving the authenticity of their origins, despite the restaurant's ever-growing popularity and an increasingly mixed clientele.

Not forgetting

■ **Al Regno di Re Ferdinando II (90)** Via di Monte Testaccio 39 – 00153 Rome ☎ (06) 5783725 ➟ (06) 57285389 Neapolitan cuisine ●● *The full range of Neapolitan cookery, from working-class recipes to dishes fit for a banquet at the Bourbon court: an experience not to be missed.*

■ **Osteria dei Tempi Nostri (91)** Via Luca della Robbia 34 – 00153 Rome ☎ (06) 57300685 Roman cuisine ● *A relaxed atmosphere in which to enjoy delicate crêpes and a vast selection of cold dishes matched by a good choice of wines.*

■ **Turiddo (92)** Via Galvani 64 – 00153 Rome ☎ (06) 5750447 Roman cuisine ● *The style of cuisine, atmosphere and prices all seem caught in a time-warp. Ideal for devotees of the neo-realism of the immediate post-war period!*

bonus in the evenings is the host of local night spots in the vicinity.
■ After dark ➡ 78 ➡ 82 ➡ 86

90

89

87

87

This Neapolitan restaurant is a temple of regional cookery. According to the sign at the entrance: 'You are now leaving the Papal States and entering the realm of King Ferdinand!'

Al Regno di Re Ferdinando II

88

Testaccio

This is the prime district for late-night entertainment. People are about until the small hours, and you will also find many places not mentioned in this guide.

After dark

Piazze

Going out in Rome may simply mean meeting friends in the squares of the city center, where life goes on into the early hours. The Piazza del Panteon is for the younger generation, while late-night diners converge on the Campo dei Fiori ➥ 36; stroll in Piazza Navona, where fortune-tellers ply their trade every evening.

Rome in summer

In July and August, seating for 2,500 people and two giant screens are installed in the church of Santi Giovanni e Paolo and at the Antiquarium for a film festival. During the same period, many events are staged in the area around the Basilica di Massenzio.
Ente Provinciale per il Turismo di Roma, Via Parigi 11 ☎ (06) 488991

38 Nights out

THE INSIDER'S FAVORITES

Reservations

The *Prontobiglietto* service enables you to reserve seats for the theater by telephone. The tickets (10% supplement) have to be picked up at an agency.
Box Office *Viale Giulio Cesare 88*
☎ (06) 52200342
Mon. 3.30–5pm; Wed.–Fri. 10am–1pm, 2.30–5pm; Sat. 10am–1pm
Gesman 92 *Via Angelo Emo 65*
☎ (06) 39740789
Mon.–Fri. 9am–1pm, 2–6pm; Sat. 9am–1pm

INDEX BY AREA

The Romans are great lovers of opera, the theater and concerts. As regular subscribers, they snaffle nearly all the available seats, which makes it difficult, if not impossible, for the occasional spectator to get a ticket. Patience is called for, but do not forget that Rome is big and lively enough to offer a whole range of less 'official' activities, many of which

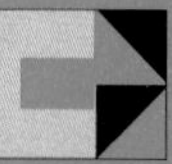

After dark

Argentina (1)

Largo di Torre Argentina 52 – 00196 Rome
☎ (06) 68804601 / 2 ➟ (06) 6877396

64, 70, 87, 492 Largo di Torre Argentina **Box office** *Mon.–Sat. 10am–2pm, 3–7pm* **Performances** *Mon., Wed., Fri.–Sat. 9pm; Thurs., Sun. 5pm* ● *30,000–50,000 lire*

This magnificent 'entertainment machine', built in the early 18th century, is unequaled for staging big and complex productions. For almost three hundred years, it has hosted the capital's most celebrated dramatic, operatic and musical creations. It is now the headquarters of the Teatro di Roma, whose program is devoted exclusively to drama, both home-grown productions and productions staged in conjunction with other state-funded Italian theaters.

Sistina (2)

Via Sistina 129 – 00187 Rome ☎ (06) 4826841 ➟ (06) 485986

M *A Barberini* **Box office** *Mon.–Sun. 10am–1pm, 3.30–7pm* **Performances** *Tues.–Sat. 9pm; Sun. 5pm* ● *33,000–70,000 lire*

The few Italian musicals that have won fame abroad originated at the Sistina, an essential venue for any musical production wanting to make it big in Rome. The program is extremely varied but, probably on account of the auditorium's perfect acoustics, it tends to be dominated by recitals given by great actors, artists, singers and musicians.

are just as entertaining and rewarding. Consult *Trovaroma*, the entertainment supplement published by *La Repubblica*.

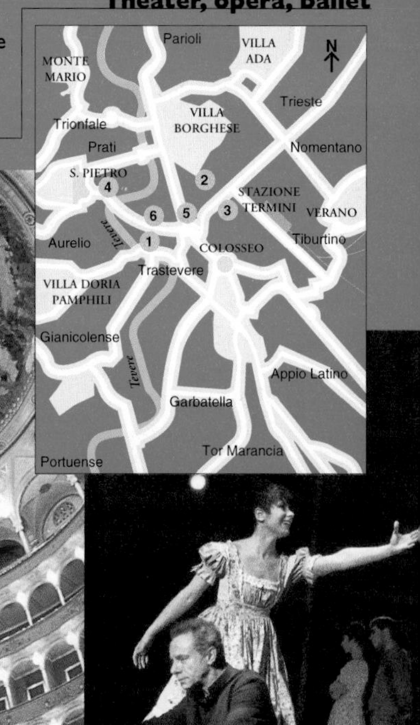

Teatro dell'Opera (3)

Piazza B. Gigli – 00184 Rome ☎ (06) 481601 ➟ (06) 4881253

M *A Repubblica* ⏲ ***Box office*** *Tues.–Sat. 9am–8pm* ***Performances*** *variable* ● *30,000–165,000 lire* Y

During the first half of the 20th century, this was one of Italy's most prestigious opera houses, but it then went into a long decline that lasted until quite recently. Now it has risen from its ashes, urged on by the general desire to restore the capital's fortunes in all the arts, including opera and ballet. The opera season proper begins in January, but many high-quality concerts and recitals are produced from October to December.

Not forgetting

■ **Auditorio dell'Accademia Nazionale di Santa Cecilia (4)** Via della Conciliazione 4 – 00193 Rome ☎ (06) 6780742 *The international prestige of this institution is evident from its program: there is a rapid turnover of conductors, soloists, ensembles and orchestras from all parts of the world, as if they were competing for the honor of performing in this auditorium!*
■ **Quirino (5)** Via Minghetti 1 – 00187 Rome ☎ (06) 6794585 ➟ (06) 6791346 *Inaugurated in 1871, this theater still has a great fascination for Italian actors, drama companies and producers wanting to make their reputation as exponents of the classical repertoire.* ■ **Valle (6)** Via del Teatro Valle 23/a – 00186 Rome ☎ (06) 6869049 ➟ (06) 6892010 *This little jewel of a theater, dating from the 18th century, specializes in remakes of the great classics.*

Rome's musical life can be a confusing mixture, with very few venues devoted to a single form of entertainment. Cabaret, for example, tends to be featured only on two or three evenings a week, or is relegated to a small room in a much larger musical complex. This is surprising when one considers that the Roman school of cabaret has produced some

After dark

Alfellini (7)

Via Carletti 5 – 00154 Rome ☎ (06) 5757570

B Piramide *Tues.–Sun. 8pm–2am* ● *Tues.–Thurs, Sun. 25,000 lire; Fri., Sat. 30,000 lire*

At the end of World War II, American soldiers would come here to listen to good jazz and swing and feel nostalgic for home. Since those days the club has changed its name and style a number of times. It is now the favorite *rendezvous* of those who like to share in the fun with up-and-coming young performers. Audience participation is encouraged. In other words, they will attempt to get you up on stage. Reminiscent of an old factory, and unusually large for cabaret acts, this venue has witnessed the first steps of many movie and television stars.

Alpheus (8)

Via del Commercio 36 – 00154 Rome
☎ (06) 5747826 ➠ (06) 5747827

B Piramide *Tues.–Sun. 10pm–3am* ● *Tues.–Thurs, Sun. 10,000 lire (drink included); Fri. 15,000 lire (drink included); Sat. 15,000 lire (no drink)*

The Alpheus is Rome's biggest late-night entertainment 'factory'. It consists of three large auditoria with a total floor area of over 21,500 square feet, each with its own specialty: live and disco music, concerts (often star-studded affairs) and cabaret. The cabaret performances are popular and extremely diverse, even including spectacular exhibitions of belly-dancing! You can eat in a separate restaurant area, where pizzas and Arab-style dishes are served. The ideal place if you have no definite idea how you want to spend an evening: here you can switch from one type of entertainment to another.

Bistrot les Artistes (9)

Via Montecchi 6 – 00153 Rome ☎ (06) 5814308

44, 75, 170 Viale di Trastevere *Tues.–Sun. 9pm–2am* ● *entry free of charge*

A tiny venue devoted exclusively to cabaret on what is billed as the world's smallest stage! Every square inch and every moment of the evening is packed with drama. Newcomers and those excluded from the official circuits are welcome here, so regular cabaret performers often alternate with mime and street artists. Hot and cold food is served, and there is an excellent wine list.

Not forgetting

■ **Hollywood Club (10)** Via Bettolo 33 – 00195 Rome ☎ (06) 3701183 *Each evening is a side-splitting parody of Oscar Night, in which the audience is invited to participate and steals the show.*

■ **Down Town (11)** Via dei Marsi 17 – 00185 Rome ☎ (06) 3701952 *Young people come here to applaud the young hopefuls of Italian cabaret. There is a show every evening except Saturday, which is devoted to live music.*

top-class comedians who cut their teeth in the capital's night-spots before going on to star in movies and on television.

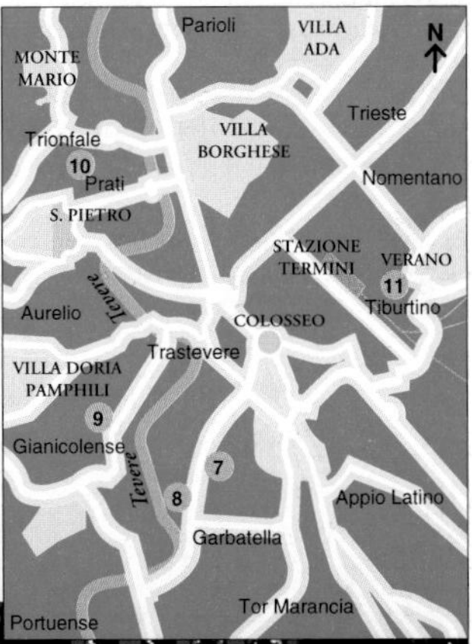

8

8

7

8

8

Rome's nightlife hardly bears comparison with that of London or New York, but in the city's basements lovers of good music and discerning observers will be aware of a smoldering fire, always likely to break out and set the audience alight. There is an ever-changing galaxy of clubs, where Italian and Anglo-American groups and soloists perform to a high

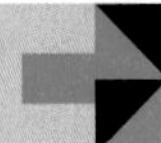

After dark

Big Mama (12)

Vicolo San Francesco a Ripa 18 – 00153 Rome
☎ (06) 5812551 / 5806497

44, 75, 170 Viale di Trastevere *Tues.–Sat. 9pm–1.30am* ● *monthly membership card 10,000 lire; annual membership card 20,000 lire*

This is a temple of blues and a must for lovers of excellence. There is a full program of top-class concerts, featuring the great names of international blues and jazz, and the best Italian performers. Giorgia's extraordinary talent and vitality was nurtured here. Every evening the Big Mama is packed with a relaxed audience of 30 to 40 year-olds, enjoying the music along with a fine selection of pasta dishes, *risottos* and homemade *foccaccia*. Unusually for an establishment of this kind, smoking is strictly forbidden.

Folkstudio (13)

Via Frangipane 42 – 00184 Rome
☎ (06) 4871063 ➠ (06) 4820732

M *B Cavour* *Tues.–Sun. 9.30–11.30pm* ● *annual membership card 5,000 lire; concerts 10,000–20,000 lire*

A legendary venue in the 1960s and '70s, Folkstudio has always been famous for musical research and experimentation, which soon earned it a reputation as a center of 'underground' music. Such stars as Francesco de Gregori and Antonello Venditti made their début here. The present fashion is for all forms of acoustic music, with theme evenings devoted mainly to British and American artists. The room is Spartan and there is no bar: this place is for music and nothing else.

Akab (14)

Via di Monte Testaccio 69 – 00153 Rome
☎ (06) 5744154

M *B Piramide* *Mon.–Sat. 10pm–4am* ● *15,000–25,000 lire (drink included)*

You have to stand in line to get into this former factory in the Testaccio district, now transformed into a concert hall devoted to everything new, experimental and switched on. The constant quest for new forms of expression has won it a national reputation. The predominantly punkish young people who come here (20 to 30 year-olds) are restrained and attentive during concerts, quite wild when the dancing begins.

Not forgetting

■ **Clochard (15)** Via del Teatro Pace 29/30 – 00186 Rome ☎ (06) 68802029 *Friendly, good-natured atmosphere in this night club packed with young people. Funky, disco and revival music, excellent drinks and a good restaurant.*
■ **Fonclea (16)** Via Crescenzio 82/a – 00193 Rome ☎ (06) 6896302 *A relaxed club specializing in live music, where you can have a meal and drink some fine Scotch and Irish whiskies.*

standard. Meanwhile African and Latin-American music is constantly gaining ground.

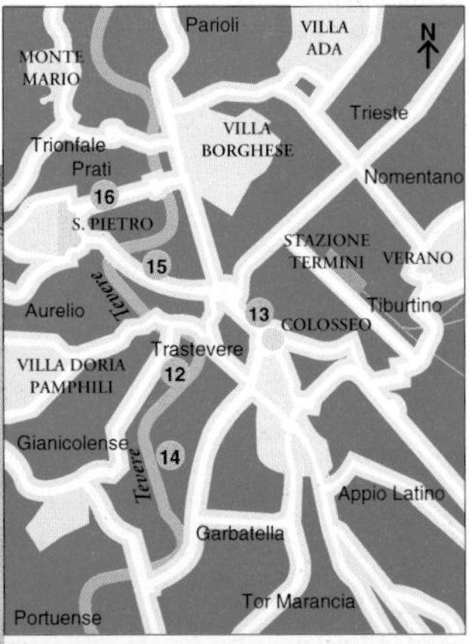

12

13

14

12

14

Where can you go for a drink? Rome offers a wide range of bars and discos, each with a distinct personality. They differ in the type of service, opening hours, prices, and kind of entertainment. In some disco bars you will find live music, and there are cocktail bars where everyone drinks beer! Some have restaurant facilities, others dance floors. They do have

After dark

Jazz Café (17)

Via Zanardelli 12 – 00186 Rome ☎ ➟ (06) 6861990

70, 87, 492 Via Zanardelli ***Cocktail bar*** *Daily 10.30pm–3am*

Huge, elegant, chic, extremely popular with young people in their twenties, this is one of Rome's most attractive and trendy cocktail bars. Founded by Jeff Blynn, one of the impresarios of Roman nightlife, the Jazz Café opens and closes late. There are two rooms, with quite distinct personalities. Upstairs you can drink and chat while listening to good music at a modest decibel level. Downstairs, bands create a more lively atmosphere, though never excessively so. But the pleasant ambiance comes at a price: undesirables are courteously but firmly turned away at the entrance.

Bar del Fico (18)

Piazza del Fico 26/28 – 00186 Roma ☎ (06) 6865205

62, 64 Corso Vittorio Emanuele II ; 70, 87 Corso del Rinascimento ***Cocktail bar*** *Mon.–Sat. 8am–2am; Sun. 1pm–2am*

Strollers on the Piazza del Fico, which owes its name to a frail fig-tree planted nearby, always end up sitting at one of the tables of this former cafeteria, which at first glance is no different from others of its kind. And yet, there is a constant coming and going of customers – actors, artists, politicians and celebrities of all sorts – irresistibly drawn by the typically Roman atmosphere which pervades the Piazza Navona and neighboring streets. You cannot but feel nostalgia for lost childhood as you contemplate the selection of homemade cakes.

The Drunken Ship (19)

Piazza Campo de' Fiori 20 – 00186 Rome ☎ (06) 68300535

62, 64 Corso Vittorio Emanuele II ***Disco bar*** *Mon.–Sat. 6pm–2am; Sun. 10am–2am* ***Brunch*** *Sun. noon–3pm*

Every evening this disco bar seems to suck in, like a sponge, the crowds of young people of all origins and nationalities crossing the splendid Campo dei Fiori. The bare-brick walls and arches contribute to the relaxed atmosphere of this improvised theater, where lively jam sessions are always in progress. At dusk, when the time comes for the evening aperitif, everything springs to life. In fine weather, this is a good place to lounge at the tables outside and enjoy watching the ever-changing kaleidoscope of people strolling in the square.

Not forgetting

■ **Wild West Saloon (20)** Via Sardegna 27 – 00187 Rome ☎ (06) 482188 Disco bar *Four large rooms with wild-west décor, where music lovers, the hungry, the thirsty, and* salsa *and* meringue *aficionados will all find their heart's desire.*

■ **It (21)** Via degli Avignonesi 19 – 00187 Disco bar *Popular with young people, relaxed atmosphere. Mobile phones are banned. One room in which to have a drink and a chat, and two others for dancing and listening to the music.*

one or two points in common: there is no age barrier, and all are packed until late at night.

17

18

19

19

THE DRUNKEN SHIP 96-97

17

19

Piano bars are something of a Roman institution – quiet, reassuring places to spend a relaxed evening sipping cocktails. Elsewhere electronic keyboards may have usurped the place of the traditional grand piano, but here it still reigns supreme. Do not forget, though, that appearances are important, so dress for the occasion. Some establishments may even

After dark

22 23 24 23

Tartarughino (22)

Via della Scrofa 1 – 00186 Rome ☎ (06) 6864131

70, 87 Via di Ripetta *Mon.–Sat. 9pm–4am*

The Tartarughino has been going strong for twenty years, unaffected by fashion and the changing fortunes of the financiers and politicians who have made it their regular haunt. Elegant and discreet, it seems to measure time by changes in government, rather than the changing years. The setting is conservative and strictly formal, but the atmosphere is enlivened by an excellent pianist who draws on a repertoire of popular tunes going back to the 1970s, with obvious appeal for the over-forties. It is not uncommon for someone to burst into song and give a sparkling solo performance.

Jonathan's Angels (23)

Via della Fossa 16 – 00186 Rome ☎ (06) 6893426

62, 64 Corso Vittorio Emanuele II ; 70, 87 Corso del Rinascimento *Mon. 8pm–2am; Tues.–Sun. 4pm–2am*

Just off the Piazza Navona ➡ 118, this is a must if you want the full picture of Roman nightlife. The setting is delightful, decorated with a jumble of pictures, *objets d'art* and sculptures, which give the place an inimitable vitality. The music is exactly what you would expect of a traditional piano bar, though the personality of individual musicians ensures that it is never stale or dull.

require you to produce an invitation or letter of introduction.

Spago (24)

Via di Monte Testaccio 35 – 00153 Rome ☎ (06) 5744999

M *B Piramide* ⏲ *Tues.–Sat. 11pm–3am* ● *first drink 15,000 lire*

This establishment caters for a sophisticated, select clientele. There are two distinct areas: the first accommodates the piano bar and groups specializing in soul, funk, dance music and hits from the 1970s; the second is more of a disco bar, with music suited to an intimate evening with your partner or a group of friends. Be warned, though: to be allowed across the threshold of the Spago, you need to be smartly dressed.

Not forgetting

■ **L'Albicocca (25)** Piazza Cavour 17/c – 00193 Rome ☎ (06) 3212498 *1970s atmosphere and chic décor. The languorous South-American music favored by the pianist has romantic appeal for those in their forties.*

■ **L'Atleta (26)** Via dei Genovesi 31 – 00153 Rome ☎ (06) 5896689 *A quiet, traditional place to spend a relaxed, romantic evening. The music is good and tasty snacks are served.*

Birrerie (pub-style bars) are the latest development in Roman nightlife. After a cautious trial period, they are multiplying at an astonishing rate, with no loss in popularity. Most resemble British or Irish pubs, but scratch a bit and you will find that each has its own style, depending very much on the inventiveness of the owners. One may specialize in

After dark

Abbey Theatre (27)

Via del Governo Vecchio 51 – 00186 Rome
☎ (06) 6861341 ➟ (06) 6798894

62, 64 Corso Vittorio Emanuele II ; 70, 87 Corso del Rinascimento *Mon.–Thurs 9.30am–1am; Fri.–Sat. 9.30am–2am; Sun. 6pm–1am*

The labyrinthine layout gives this pub a curious atmosphere, though its décor and the food and drink on offer are otherwise very traditional. There is a good choice of beers and whiskies, and an interesting selection of cold foods. It often organizes parties, and Irish evenings with live music by visiting groups.

Crazy Bull (28)

Via Mantova 5/b – 00198 Rome ☎ (06) 3338432 ➟ (06) 3338433

490, 495 Porta Pia *Daily 7.30pm–2am*

A Wild-West-style saloon, where crowds of young people wander from room to room to a sound track engineered by a smart DJ. The kitchens supply a rapid succession of hamburgers and steaks, and also some tasty surprises, such as green-tomato fritters.

Bandana Republic (29)

Via Alessandria 44 – 00198 Rome ☎ (06) 44249751

490, 495 Porta Pia *Mon.–Sat. 12.30pm–3pm, 7.30pm–2am; Sun. 7.30pm–2am*

Small, crowded and full of smoke. If there was fog outside, you could believe you were in Glasgow or Liverpool. The carefully crafted atmosphere is matched by an excellent selection of beers and Scotch and

bagpipe concerts, another in quiz evenings, or even 'chat' sessions on the Internet. People have responded with enthusiasm.

28

30

29

28

29

Irish whiskies. The menu strikes a more Mediterranean note: *panini*, good salads, and some highly imaginative dishes.

Victoria House (30)

Via di Gesù e Maria – 00187 Rome ☎ (06) 3201698

A Flaminio *Mon.–Sat. 6pm–1.30am; Sun. 5pm–0.30am*

The fact that English, Scottish and Irish visitors to Rome make a bee-line for this pub should be a guarantee of authenticity. Is it the care with which the décor has been put together, the choice of beers and whiskies, or the know-how of the staff? You have only to walk through the doors to know that this is a corner of the British Isles transposed to Rome.

Not forgetting

Mad Jack (31) Via Arenula 20 – 00186 Rome ☎ (06) 68808223
Some well-chosen antiques add to the warmth of this strictly Irish pub. An open, spacious atmosphere is created by the many windows giving onto the street.

The Albert (32) Via del Traforo 132 – 00187 Rome ☎ (06) 4818795
The most 'British' of Rome's pubs, with tasteful furniture imported from the United Kingdom. Pleasant atmosphere and a wide range of beers to accompany generous salads and snacks of all kinds.

Strange to say, Rome's discos have not followed the trend apparent in other parts of Italy, where informality has penetrated even the corridors of power, but continue to promote the affluent, jacket-and-tie culture of the early 1980s. The attachment to past glories is apparent in the revival of the piano bar and the organization of theme evenings with groups

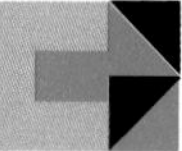

After dark

Gilda (33)

Via Mario de' Fiori 97 – 00187 Rome
☎ (06) 6784838 ➠ (06) 6780547

A Spagna *Tues.–Sun. 11pm–4am* ● *40,000 lire* *9.30pm–midnight*

The most fashionable of Rome's night clubs, a magnet for those who want to see and be seen, including politicians and show-business celebrities. Its great strength is the spacious, comfortable discotheque, generously furnished with soft couches. The piano bar is hardly less popular, and always packed.

Angelo Azzurro (34)

Via Cardinale Merry del Val 13 – 00153 Rome ☎ (06) 5800472

44, 75, 170 Viale di Trastevere *Tues.–Thurs 7pm–1am ~ Fri.–Sun. midnight–4am* ● *Fri., Sun. entry free of charge; Sat. 15,000 lire*

This gay club caused a scandal when it opened in the 1970s. But its founders knew what they were doing. Twenty years later, the Angelo Azzurro is still in vogue, welcoming gays and non-gays attracted by music played by some of the capital's best DJs.

Alibi (35)

Via di Monte Testaccio 40 – 00153 Rome ☎ / ➠ (06) 5743448

B Piramide *Wed.–Sun. 11.30pm–4am* ● *Wed., Fri., Sat. 15,000 lire; Thurs., Sun. admission free*

Founded as a place of freedom for the gay community, this disco has two big rooms and a splendid terrace for the summer months. Nowadays the relaxed atmosphere attracts revelers regardless of gender, age, culture and appearance. The talented DJs who orchestrate the dancing manage to marry new trends with oldies from the 1960s and 70s.

Bella Blu (36)

Via L. Luciani 21 – 00197 Rome
☎ (06) 3230490 – 3218749 ➠ (06) 3226345

52, 926 Viale Buozzi *Tues.–Sun. 11.30pm–3.30am* ● *40,000 lire*

The Bella Blu may no longer be the shining star of Roman nightlife, but it is still a good place for those who prefer intimacy to noise, dancing to jigging around, conversation to restless agitation. In short, a disco for 40-year-olds who appreciate elegance and the quality of the drinks.

Not forgetting

■ **Notorius (37)** Via San Nicola da Tolentino 22 – 00187 Rome ☎ (06) 4746888 *This tiny, traditional disco is frequented by people from the world of cinema and members of the international jet-set passing through Rome.*

■ **Piper (38)** Via Tagliamento 9 – 00198 Rome ☎ (06) 8414459 *Still in fashion, this historic club attracts the young and the less young, who mix in a relaxed, casual atmosphere.*

reworking the big hits of the 1970s and 80s.

34

35

33

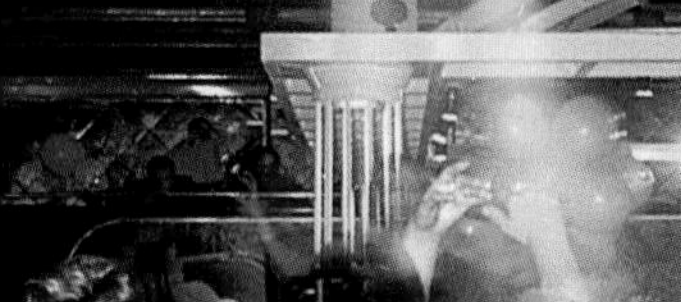

35

36

What to see

Rome by bus
For 10, 000 lire, a n°.110 bus will take you on an interesting three-hour tour of the city. Leaving from Termini railroad station ➡ 12, it follows a circular route taking in Piazza Barberini, Piazzale Flaminio, Saint Peter's ➡ 108, Piazza Venezia ➡ 94, the Colosseum ➡ 100 and San Giovanni in Laterano ➡ 104.

Sung masses
Jan. 25
San Paolo fuori le Mura
June 24
San Giovanni in Laterano ➡ 104
June 29
St. Peter's ➡ 108 (choir of the Sistine Chapel)
Dec. 31
Te Deum in the Church of the Gesù ➡ 94

A spectacular evening out

The *Comune di Roma* (city administration) organizes *son et lumière* evenings in the imperial forums for groups of between 30 and 50 persons (days and times vary). The program also includes a guided tour (in English). An unforgettable experience, but be sure to book ahead.
Sinfonie di luce ☎ *(06) 48882501* ⏲ *Mon.–Fri. 10am-5pm* ● *12, 000 lire*

THE INSIDER'S FAVORITES

INDEX BY TYPE

Roman postcards: the geometric paving of the Piazza del Campidoglio (Capitol), designed by Michelangelo (1); Bernini's Fontana della Barcaccia and the church of Trinità dei Monti (2); the giant amphitheater of the Colosseum, symbol of Rome (3); the Capitoline She-Wolf (4); one of the Villa Borghese fountains (5); the Pincio belvedere (6); the Pantheon (7);

What to see

1 2 5 6 7

Nearly everywhere people make a distinction between history and myth... except perhaps in Rome. In the Eternal City, the two are inextricably mixed. Modern Rome is a capital city caught between its past – less remote than is commonly believed – and the insistent knocking of the third millennium, about to be celebrated with a Jubilee year. A power center which became the capital of Italy without experiencing the proud freedom of the medieval city states (a paradox which other cities enviously thrust in its face), a gigantic catalog of Mediterranean civilization compiled in a state of feverish delirium, Rome is one big museum, indoors and out. It rises on its seven hills, disappears into the bowels of its catacombs, marches to the rhythm of its metaphysical population of obelisks, columns and talking statues, stifles in its choked streets, and delights in its magically silent backwaters. It shamelessly casts its elegance in the face of its notorious indolence. It boasts of being all things to all men: the throne of Saint Peter, the scene of the austere Christianity of the early centuries, the baroque extravagance of Bernini and Borromini, the discoveries of Renaissance man, and the crucible of its illustrious victims, from Giordano Bruno to Galileo. It adorns itself in the green of its gardens, the white and pink of its marbles, the yellow and red of its houses, the gray of its stones, the muddy yellow of its river, and the blue of the water that spurts from its fountains. It feeds hungrily on the admiration of its tourists, happy in the conviction that they are discovering something already contemplated by millions, and of its famous visitors, for whom it provides abundant material for rapturous celebration.

Palazzo del Quirinale, the presidential palace (8); Ponte Sant'Angelo and the dome of St Peter's (9); the Via Appia Antica (10).

Over the centuries, Rome has been worshipped like no other city, welcoming an uninterrupted stream of pilgrims. But if Rome has always specialized in the art of illusion, the Romans themselves were never taken in. Until not long ago, they found it amusing to play a game of philosophical *trompe l'œil*: accustomed to living in the midst of churches which resemble palaces, and palaces which resemble triumphal arches, they always managed to give the impression they knew what was truth and what was illusion. But in recent times the city, wrestling with the thousand-and-one problems that confront a modern metropolis, and prisoner of a cultural heritage that defies its administrators, has begun to confuse even those who thought they could distinguish history from myth. For instance, faced with the tricky question: 'How did Rome come into existence?' – which every primary school teacher continues to ask his or her pupils – Romans would reply with a slightly self-satisfied air that the city originated with the gradual merging of a number of proto-historic villages around the Palatine, the largest and most strategic of its seven hills. This answer, enthusiastically endorsed by the primary school teacher, represented the well-deserved triumph of the goddess Reason, supported by her faithful handmaid archeology, over the darkness of mythology. Archeology could boast of having at last erased the furrow plowed by Romulus and the ritual sacrifice of his brother Remus, relegating them to the cobwebby world of fable. But recently archeology has betrayed her goddess, announcing the discovery of a stratum which corresponds to Romulus's furrow. You can never really trust historical scholarship in Rome. Too many fables turn out to be true.

In the area

Citadel and religious center since classical times (the Temple of Jupiter, Rome's largest temple was erected here in 509 BC), the Campidoglio, or Capitol, has always been the heart of the city. It still plays an important role in the life of the capital, as seat of the main civic institutions. Its two

What to see

Piazza del Campidoglio (1)

46, 86, 181, 628, 710, 719 Via del Teatro di Marcello

This was Rome's first modern square, planned as a great terrace overlooking the city. When Charles V visited Rome in 1536, Pope Paul III commissioned Michelangelo to create a complex worthy of the seat of the papacy. The equestrian statue of Marcus Aurelius (the original of which is now in the Capitoline Museum) was the central feature around which he drew up his plans for this trapezoid 'square'.

Palazzo Senatorio (2)
Piazza del Campidoglio – 00186 Rome

46, 86, 181, 628, 710, 719 Via del Teatro di Marcello

Now the town hall, this building was designed by Giacomo della Porta and Girolamo Rainaldi (1605); Michelangelo planned the double flight of steps adorned with statues representing the Nile and the Tiber. The left-hand wing of the building contains Martin V's tower (1582).

Musei Capitolini (3)
Piazza del Campidoglio – 00186 Rome ☎ (06) 67102071

46, 86, 181, 628, 710, 719 Via del Teatro di Marcello *Tues.–Sun. 9am–7pm*
● *10,000 lire (access only to the Conservatori apartments and the Capitoline Museum itself)*

The Capitoline museum, which is the oldest in Europe (1471), and the Palazzo dei Conservatori house magnificent collections of classical artefacts (the celebrated *Capitoline She-Wolf*, the colossal *Head of Constantine*, the *Dying Gaul*, and countless busts of emperors and famous people) and some of the great works of 16th- and 17th-century European painting (Titian, Veronese, Rubens, Caravaggio, Guido Reni). The museum has been restructured, and in 1997 new exhibition rooms were opened in the former Montemartini prison.

Santa Maria in Aracoeli (4)
Piazza del Campidoglio 4 – 00186 Rome ☎ (06) 6798155

46, 86, 181, 628, 710, 719 Via del Teatro di Marcello *Daily 6.30am–6pm*
● *admission free*

According to legend, the Virgin and the Infant Jesus appeared to the Emperor Augustus, who built an altar on this spot. In the 13th century the Franciscans erected the present building, which became the official church of the Roman city government. There are works by Donatello, Pietro Cavallini and Benozzo Gozzoli, and the chapel of San Bernardino of Siena is decorated with frescos by Pinturicchio (1486).

Not forgetting

■ **Santi Luca e Martina (5)** on the corner of Via del Tulliano – 00186 Rome *Despite its sober decoration, this is one of the most exquisite of Rome's 17th-century churches. Restored by Pietro da Cortona in 1634, it is currently closed for another round of restoration work.*

high points, the Capitolium and the Arx, are separated by a hollow which now forms the Piazza del Campidoglio.

1

2

3

On the Piazza del Campidoglio stands a copy of the equestrian statue of Marcus Aurelius.

4

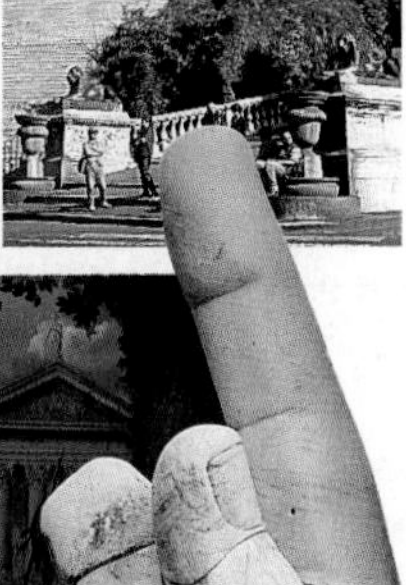

3

In the area

The wide streets which converge on Piazza Venezia make it one of the noisiest and most congested places in Rome, but the adjacent buildings are world famous. Its present appearance is largely due to developments dating from the end of the last century and the Fascist era.

What to see

Vittoriano (6)
Piazza Venezia – 00186 Rome

46 Via San Marco ; 44, 181, 710, 719 Via del Teatro di Marcello

Erected in the years 1885–1911 as a memorial to Victor Emmanuel II (1820–78), Italy's first king. Criticized for the 'nordic' whiteness of the marble, and threatened with destruction by Mussolini, this monument has attracted some most unflattering nicknames: 'Italy's biggest urinal', and 'the typewriter'.

Palazzo di Venezia (7)
Piazza Venezia 3 – 00186 Rome

46 Via San Marco **Museum** *Via del Plebiscito 118 – 00186 Rome ☎ (06) 6798865 Tues.–Sat. 9am–2pm; Sun. and public holidays 9am–1pm ● 8,000 lire*

Pietro Barbo, the future Pope Paul II (1464), had this palace built when he was appointed cardinal of San Marco in 1451. The work continued after his death and was completed in the 16th century. It is now a museum, housing fine collections of painting, porcelain, sculpture and jewelry from various periods.

Basilica di San Marco (8)
Piazza di San Marco 48 – 00186 Rome ☎ (06) 6795205

46 Via San Marco Daily 8.30am–12.30pm, 4pm–7pm ● admission free

Founded in AD 336 by St Marcus, this basilica was incorporated by Pope Paul II into the new Palazzo di Venezia, in the 15th century. ★ Do not miss the Romanesque campanile, the coffered ceiling decorated with the papal coat of arms, or the medieval apse mosaic, modeled on that of the church of Santi Cosma e Damiano.

Chiesa del Gesù (9)
Piazza del Gesù e Via degli Astalli 16 – 00186 Rome ☎ (06) 697001

56, 64, 70, 492, 186, 710 Via del Plebiscito Daily 6am–12.30pm, 4–7.30pm ● admission free

The main Jesuit church in Rome, in structure and decoration the Gesù was the prototype of Counter-Reformation church buildings. The architects were Jacopo Vignola and Giacomo della Porta, while Andrea Pozzo created the sumptuous chapel dedicated to Saint Ignatius, the founder of the order.

Not forgetting

■ **Colonna Traiana (10)** Piazza Santa Maria di Loreto – 00186 Rome ☎ (06) 6790048 *The relief sculptures on Trajan's column are arranged in a continuous spiral 656 ft long. They tell of the emperor's victorious campaign against the Dacians.* ■ **Foro e Mercati di Traiano (11)** Via IV Novembre 94 – 00186 Rome ☎ (06) 6790048 *Trajan built Rome's largest forum (AD 107–113) and the markets named after him. The architect was Apollodorus of Damascus.* ■ **Foro di Augusto (12)** Via IV Novembre 94 and Piazza del Grillo – 00186 Rome ☎ (06) 6790048 *The second of the imperial forums, with temple dedicated to Mars Ultor.* ■ **Santi Domenico e Sisto (13)** Largo Angelicum 1 – 00186 Rome ☎ (02) 67021 *The monumental entrance to this baroque church (closed to the public) is reached by a double circular staircase.*

Piazza Venezia
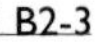
E B2-3

Where to stay ➥ 38

Via del Plebiscito
Piazza Venezia
P.za d. Gesù
V. d. Astalli
V. Ara Coeli
V. S. Marco
Piazza S. Marco
V. S. Eufemia
Via IV Novembre
VILLA ALDOBRANDINI
V. dei Fori Imperiali
Via Alessandrina
Sal. d. Grillo
N
7
8
9
6
10
11
12
57

6

0

2

1

9

In the area

This archeological site bears witness to the twelve centuries of history that forged Roman civilization. During the Republic (4th–1st centuries BC), the Forum was the political, religious and commercial center of the city, while the Palatine, originally settled by Romulus, was the hill on which the emperors

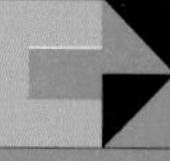

What to see

22

14

27

Foro Romano (14-24)

Via dei Fori Imperiali e Piazza Santa Maria Nova – 00186 Rome ☎ (06) 6990110

B Colosseo ⏲ *summer: daily 9am–6pm / winter: Mon.–Sat 9am–3pm; Sun. and public holidays 9am–1pm* ● *admission free* *(Entrance opposite the subway station)*

Each monument or area in the Roman Forum had its own special function, civic or religious. To the first category belong the basilicas, vast covered halls divided by columns into several areas which housed the law courts and political and economic activities. Note the Basilica Æmilia (14), the last vestige of republican architecture, and the later Basilica of Maxentius and Constantine, which was a source of inspiration for many Renaissance architects. The Comitium (15) was the area where people gathered to hear the magistrates deliver speeches from a dais, known as the Rostra. On the other side, the Comitium adjoins the Curia (16), where the Senate used to meet (it was rebuilt in its present form by Diocletian, in the 3rd century). Some of the main places of worship in the forum were the Temple of Saturn (498 BC) (18), consecrated to the god who, according to tradition, had founded a city on the Capitoline Hill; the Temple of the Dioscuri (20), dedicated to the mysterious horsemen who led the Romans to victory against the people of Latium; the Temple of Vesta (21), which housed the sacred flame, tended by six vestal virgins; and finally the Temple of Antoninus and Faustina (22), which dates from AD 141 and was converted into a church in the 8th century. In imperial times, the Forum (19) was enriched with monuments to the various emperors, for instance the imposing Arch of Septimius Severus (AD 203) (17), sculpted with scenes of the key events of his two victorious campaigns in the East, and the more sober Arch of Titus (24), which illustrates the triumph of Vespasian and Titus over the Jews in AD 71.

built their villas and palaces.
■ Where to eat ➥ 64

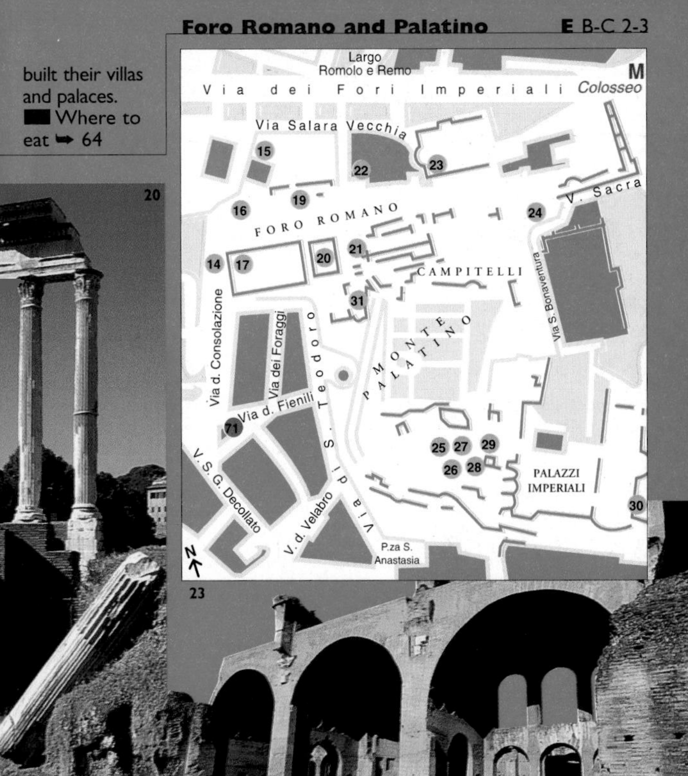

The Palatino (25-30)

Entrance in Via San Gregorio (or from the Foro Romano) – 00186 Rome ☎ (06) 6990110

M B Colosseo ⌚ summer: daily 9am–6pm / winter: Mon.–Sat. 9am–3pm; Sun. and public holidays 9am–1pm ● 12,000 lire

With its lawns and parasol pines, the Palatine is one of Rome's most magical places. During the Republic, this hill became the residential district of the Roman ruling class. The example was set by Augustus, who first decided to make it his home. The name *Palatium* came to signify both the hill and his palace. The House of Livia (25), probably reserved for his wife, and the adjacent House of Augustus (26) were decorated with sophisticated paintings in the second Pompeian style. Toward the end of the first century, the palace of Domitian was built on the central part of the hill. It consisted of the Domus Flavia (27), where public audiences were held, the Domus Augustana (29), his private residence, and the Stadium, which served as a riding school and garden. Septimius Severus enlarged the complex of buildings and created the Domus Severiana (30), from which there is a magnificent view of the Eternal City. The Antiquarium (28) houses archeological remains found on the hill: archaic artefacts, and paintings from Republican and Imperial times.

Not forgetting

■ **Santa Maria Antiqua (31)** Largo Romolo e Remo 1 – 00186 Rome ☎ (06) 6990110 *The frescos in this church (6th–9th centuries) are unique in the glimpse they give of Rome in the post-classical period.*

In the area

On the banks of the Tiber near Rome's port area, the Aventine was originally a working-class district, and a trade center. Under the Empire, it became a residential area. From its heights there is an exceptional view of the city. ■ After dark ➡ 78 ➡ 82 ■ Where to shop ➡ 162

What to see

Tempio della Fortuna Virile e Tempio di Vesta (32)

Piazza Bocca della Verità – 00186 Rome

81, 94, 160, 628, 713 Piazza Bocca della Verità

The rectangular Temple of Portunus (god of harbors), formerly known as the Temple of Fortuna Virilis, stands at the southern end of the Forum Holitorium, on the site of the old Portus Tiberinus. It was founded in the 4th or 3rd century BC, but the present building dates from the 1st century BC. Farther south, the circular temple beside the Tiber is the oldest surviving marble building in Rome. Known as the Temple of Vesta, it was in fact dedicated to Hercules. It was founded by a Roman merchant who must have become rich in the oil trade: Hercules was the patron of the oil-merchants' corporation, the *olearii.*

Santa Maria in Cosmedin (33)

Piazza Bocca della Verità 18 – 00186 Rome ☎ (06) 6781419

81, 94, 160, 628, 713 Piazza Bocca della Verità *Daily 10am–1pm, 3–6pm* ● *admission free*

Founded in the 4th century and enlarged in the 8th century by Pope Adrian I, this church was given to the Greek community living near the Tiber. It was then renamed Santa Maria in Cosmedin, after a district of Constantinople. ★ Set into the wall of the portico is the famous Bocca della Verità (Mouth of Truth), an ancient drain cover representing the god Ocean. According to legend, the jaws will snap shut over the hand of anyone telling a lie.

Santa Sabina (34)

Piazza Pietro d'Illiria 1 – 00153 Rome ☎ (06) 5743573

81, 94, 160, 628 Clivo dei Publicii *Daily 7am–1pm, 3.30–6pm* ● *admission free*

If tradition is to be believed, this church was built on the site of the house of a noblewoman, Sabina, who was converted to Christianity by one of her slaves and died during the persecutions of the Emperor Hadrian's time. Erected in the 5th century, it was remodeled several times but restored to its original form in 1914. ★ Of special interest is the magnificent cedar-wood door. The sculpted scenes include the *Israelites crossing the Red Sea* and *Christ before Pilate*. It is one of the very few examples of 5th-century Christian iconography.

Santa Cecilia (35)

Piazza di Santa Cecilia 22 – 00153 Rome ☎ (06) 5899289

23 Lungotevere Ripa ; 56, 60 Piazza G.G. Belli *Daily 10am–noon, 3–6pm* ● *admission free*

This basilica, dedicated to an early Christian martyr, was built in the 9th century during the pontificate of St Paschal I, who commissioned the apse mosaic and donated a valuable *ciborium*. In the late 13th century, Cardinal Cholet asked Pietro Cavallini to decorate the church with frescoes (only the striking *Last Judgment* now survives) and commissioned Arnolfo di Cambio to construct a new *ciborium* (1293) in the sanctuary. This is one of his finest works in Rome. Later, Stefano Maderno carved a moving statue of the saint in the position in which her body was found in 1600.

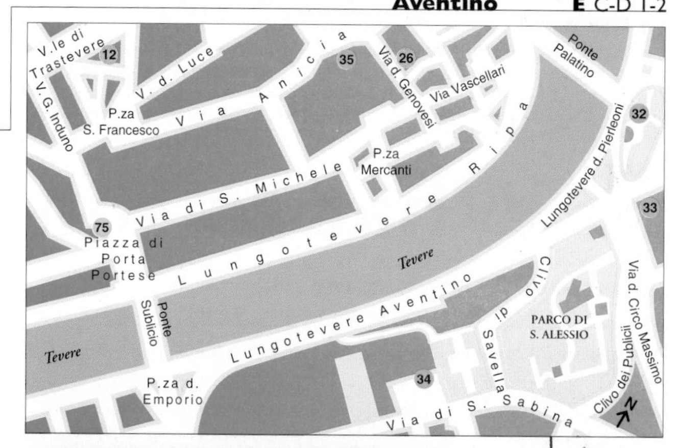

32

33

35

35

33

35

In the area

In this area are some of the most grandiose buildings of the Imperial period and three Christian sanctuaries. The Colosseum was erected on the site of the artificial lake that Nero had engineered in the grounds of his villa, the Domus Aurea. ■ Where to stay ➡ 38 ■ Where to eat ➡ 68

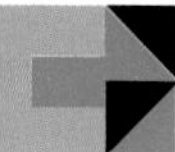

What to see

Colosseo (36)

Piazza del Colosseo – 00184 Rome ☎ (06) 7004261

M *B Colosseo* ⏲ *Mon., Tues., Thurs.–Sat. 9am–6pm; Wed., Sun. and public holidays 9am–1pm* ● *10,000 lire*

Roughly 164 ft high and 616 ft in diameter, the finest amphitheater in the Roman world was begun in AD 72, in the early years of Vespasian's reign, and finished by his son Titus. In AD 80, during an inauguration lasting a hundred days, five thousand wild animals were slaughtered! ★ The name Colosseum, first used in the Middle Ages, is thought to derive from the 114-ft-high bronze statue of Nero which stood not far away.

Arco di Costantino (37)

Piazza del Colosseo – 00184 Rome

Erected in AD 315 for Constantine's (306–37) triumphal procession after his victory over Maxentius at the Milvian Bridge (312), this is one of the largest arches to have survived the ravages of time. An imposing memorial, it is unusual in that its sculpted reliefs were 'borrowed' from a number of 2nd-century monuments.

Domus Aurea (38)

Via del Monte Oppio – 00184 Rome ☎ (06) 4872432

M *B Colosseo* ▣ *only with permission from the Soprintendenza Archeologica (antiquities department) ☎ (06) 6990110*

After his first palace was destroyed by the great fire of AD 64, Nero replaced it with an even larger building, the Domus Aurea (golden house). Every feature of the palace was a reference to the sun, with which the emperor identified himself. The surviving walls of the underground chambers, excavated in the 16th century, are decorated with arabesques and mythological figures ('grotesques'), which inspired many Renaissance artists.

San Clemente (39)

Via Labicana 95 – 00184 Rome ☎ (06) 70451018

M *B Colosseo* ⏲ *Mon.–Sat. 9am–12.30pm, 3.30–6pm; Sun. 10am–12.30pm, 3.30–6pm* ● *admission free*

A silent witness to history, no building better illustrates the superimposition of the centuries, which is one of Rome's greatest attractions. The 13th-century upper church has a baroque façade and its apse is decorated with a magnificent 12th-century mosaic, the *Triumph of the Cross*. Below is a primitive Christian church (access via the sacristy) with two fine 11th-century frescos, one of which tells the story of St Clement. This church in turn stands upon older Roman buildings!

Not forgetting

■ **San Pietro in Vincoli (40)** Piazza di San Pietro in Vincoli 4/a – 00184 Rome ☎ (06) 4882865 *As well as the chains which bound the apostle Peter when imprisoned in Jerusalem, this church contains the mausoleum of Pope Julius II.* ■ **Madonna dei Monti (41)** Via della Madonna dei Monti 41 – 00184 Rome ☎ (06) 485531 *The masterpiece of Giacomo della Porta (1580).*

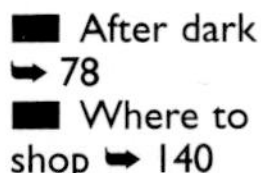
■ After dark ➥ 78
■ Where to shop ➥ 140

39

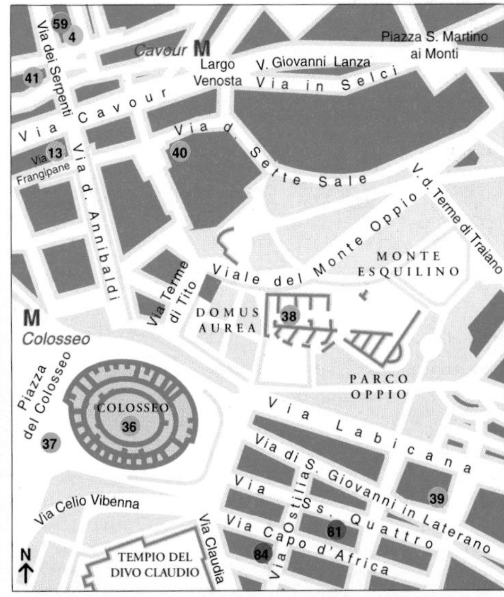

Above the tomb of Pope Julius II sits the celebrated statue of Moses, sculpted in 1513.

37

40

36

In the area

This district is the result of a long series of town-planning exercises, begun in the early 15th century and completed less than a hundred years ago. A mixture of magnificent Renaissance basilicas, classical monuments and medieval buildings. ■ Where to stay ➡ 20 ■ Where

What to see

Museo Nazionale Romano (42)

Palazzo Massimo, Piazza dei Cinquecento 67 – 00185 Rome ☎ (06) 48903500

M A, B Termini ⏲ Tues.–Sat. 9am–2pm; Sun. and public holidays 9am–1pm ● 12,000 lire; ticket also ensures admission to the Terme di Diocleziano **Palazzo Altemps** *Piazza Sant'Apollinare 46/48 ⏲ Tues.–Sun. 10am–5pm ● 10,000 lire*

The Roman national museum houses one of the world's finest collections of classical art. Its nucleus is a number of works collected in the 17th century by Cardinal Ludovisi, including the panel of the Birth of Aphrodite. The baths of Diocletian are undergoing a restructuring operation, due to be completed in December 1998. The masterpieces normally housed there have been removed to Palazzo Massimo and Palazzo Altemps.

Terme di Diocleziano (43)

Via de Nicola 79 – 00185 Rome ☎ (06) 4880530

M A Termini, Repubblica ; B Termini ⏲ Tues.–Sat. 9am–2pm; Sun. and public holidays 9am–1pm ● 12,000 lire; ticket also ensures admission to the Museo Nazionale Romano

On his return from Africa in AD 298, the Emperor Maximian ordered the building of a sumptuous complex of baths, with sporting and cultural facilities for up to 3,000 people. The baths were not completed until AD 306, after the abdication of Maximian and Diocletian.

Santa Maria degli Angeli (44)

Via Cernaia 9 – 00185 Rome ☎ (06) 4880812

M A Repubblica ⏲ Daily 7.30am–12.30pm, 4–6.30pm ● admission free

In 1561, Pope Pius IV commissioned Michelangelo to convert part of the baths of Diocletian into a church. The entrance was made in the apse of the former *caldarium*. The church was dedicated to the angels and Christian martyrs who, according to tradition, were used as slave labor in building the baths. Completed in 1749 by Vanvitelli, it is adorned with gigantic pictures, mostly transferred from St Peter's ➡ 108.

Santa Maria Maggiore (45)

Via Liberiana 27 – 00185 Rome ☎ (06) 483195

M A, B Termini ⏲ Daily 7am–6.50pm ● admission to the basilica free; loggia *frescos ● 5,000 lire*

Behind the (reworked) baroque façade of this 5th-century basilica is a wealth of art: the apse mosaics by Jacopo Torriti (1295), the *Coronation of the Virgin* in the central vaulting (12th–13th centuries), the *loggia* frescos (13th–14th centuries), and the Cappella Sistina, decorated by Domenico Fontana (1587).

Not forgetting

■ **Stazione Centrale di Termini (46)** Piazza dei Cinquecento – 00185 Rome ☎ (06) 4775 *Built 1937–1967, Rome's main station is an amalgam of Fascist and 1960s architecture.* ■ **Santa Prassede (47)** Via Santa Prassede 9/a – 00185 Rome ☎ (06) 4882456 *This early church is famous for the Carolingian mosaics which adorn the apse, choir and chapel of Saint Zeno.*

to eat ➥ 46 ■ After dark ➥ 74 ■ Where to shop ➥ 140

Santa Maria Maggiore is one of the four Roman basilicas granted the title of 'great' and enjoying the related privilege of extra-territoriality.

45

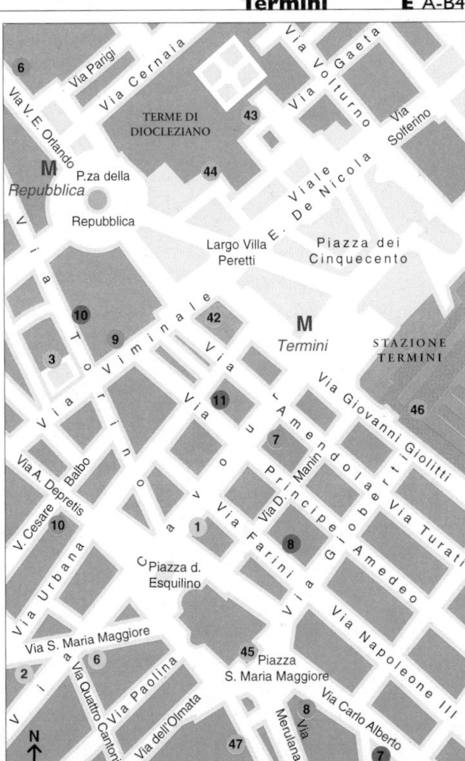

42

43

47

Because of the threat posed by the Barbarians, the Emperor Aurelian built a new city wall in the years AD 270–5. Twelve miles long, 20 ft high and 13 ft thick, defended by square towers at 100-ft intervals, the walls were reconstructed several times over the centuries. Following the line of the walls gives a sense of the extent of Rome's heritage, as most of

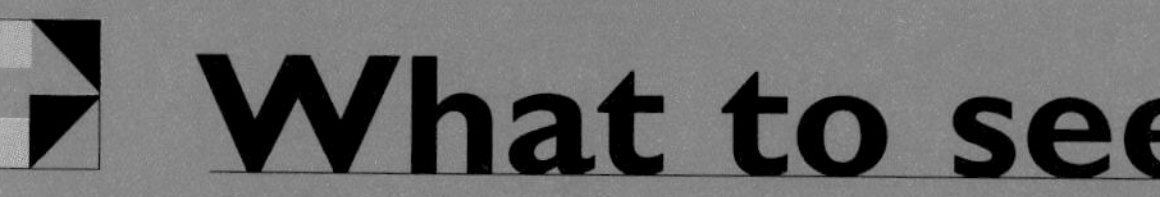

What to see

49

48

50

Sant'Agnese e Santa Costanza (48)

Via Nomentana 349 – 00162 Rome ☎ (06) 8610840

60, 36, 37, 137, 317 Via Nomentana *Daily 6.30am–noon, 4–7.45pm* ● *admission free*

This basilica, founded under Constantine (4th century) in honor of the young Christian martyr Agnes, has been remodeled several times. ★ The apse is decorated with a splendid 7th-century mosaic. From the garden there is access to the church of Santa Costanza. This was originally a mausoleum for the emperor's daughters, Constantia and Helena. Converted into a church in 1245, it still has its original 4th-century mosaics.

San Giovanni in Laterano e Battistero (49)

Piazza di San Giovanni in Laterano – 00184 Rome ☎ (06) 69886452

M *A San Giovanni* *Daily 7am–6pm* ● *admission free*

To symbolize the triumph of Christianity over paganism, Constantine built this basilica and an official residence for the popes, the *domus ecclesiae*. It is entitled 'Mother and Head of all the Churches of the City and the World'. After it was destroyed in the 14th century, rebuilding was begun in the time of Pope Sixtus V with contributions from architects Della Porta, Fontana and Borromini. Its finest features are the 16th-century carved wooden ceiling, the apse mosaic by J. Torriti and J. da Camerino (13th century) and the panels of the Porta Santa, brought from the Curia in the Forum ➡ 96. The cloisters (13th century) are remarkable for their twisted columns and inlaid mosaic work by the Cosmati family. ★ The baptistery was remodeled in 1637, but the mosaics date from the 4th–5th centuries.

the city's historic buildings are concentrated within this perimeter.

Terme di Caracalla (50)

Viale delle Terme di Caracalla 52 – 00153 Rome ☎ (06) 5758626

B Circo Massimo Tues.–Sat. 9am–5pm; Sun., Mon. and public holidays 9am–noon ● 8,000 lire

The baths played an important part in Roman social life. Built in the years AD 212–16 and in use until the end of the 6th century, the baths of Caracalla were open to the lower classes and could accommodate 1,600 bathers at any one time. They are the most monumental and best preserved of the imperial bathing establishments.

Via Appia Antica (51)

160, 628 Viale delle Terme di Caracalla ; 218 Via Appia Antica

The Via Appia, running from the Porta Capena, was begun in 312 BC to connect Rome with Brindisi. The best preserved section is beyond the Aurelian walls, near the Porta San Sebastiano. On either side of the road are tombs, catacombs and grand residences from the Imperial period.

Not forgetting

■ **San Lorenzo fuori le Mura (52)** Piazzale del Verano 3 – 00185 Rome ☎ (06) 491511 *This basilica dates from the time of Constantine and has been restored several times. It boasts works in marble by the Cosmati family, celebrated Roman craftsmen: flooring in white marble, porphyry and serpentine, ciborium, Easter candelabrum and bishop's throne.*

In the area

In Roman times, merchants drawn by the activities of the port settled on the far bank of the Tiber (Trastevere), a working-class district until the 1960s. It retains the atmosphere of a medieval village. ■ Where to eat ➡ 62 ➡ 64 ➡ 66 ■ After dark ➡ 86 ■ Where to shop ➡ 160

What to see

Santa Maria in Trastevere (53)

Via della Paglia 14/c – 00153 Rome ☎ (06) 5814802

717, 774, 780 Viale di Trastevere *Daily 8am–7pm ● admission free*

Although dating back to the 4th century, this church owes its present appearance and sumptuous apse mosaics to Pope Innocent II (12th century). The *Dormition of the Virgin* is one of the works by Pietro Cavallini (1291).

San Crisogono (54)

Piazza Sonnino 44 – 00153 Rome ☎ (06) 5818225

56, 60 Piazza G.G. Belli ; 717, 774, 780 Viale di Trastevere *Mon.–Sat. 7–11.30am, 4–7.30pm; Sun. and public holidays 8am–1pm, 4–7.30pm ● admission free*

It is difficult to imagine that behind this plain façade are to be found a pavement by the Cosmati family, fine mosaics attributed to Pietro Cavallini (13th century) and a chapel designed by Bernini!

San Pietro in Montorio (55)

Piazza di San Pietro in Montorio 2 – 00153 Rome ☎ (06) 5813940

41 Via Garibaldi *Daily 9am–noon, 4–6pm ● admission free*

The building of this church (1481–1500) was funded by their Catholic Majesties Ferdinand of Aragon and Isabella of Castille, who also commissioned Bramante to design the Tempietto, a small circular temple based on classical models. It stands to the right of the church, in the center of the cloister, on the spot where Saint Peter is believed to have been crucified.

Galleria Corsini (56)

Via della Lungara 10 – 00165 Rome ☎ (06) 68802323

23, 65, 280 Lungotevere della Farnesina *Tues.–Sat. 9am–7pm; Sun. and public holidays 9am–1pm ● 8,000 lire*

On the first floor of Palazzo Corsini is housed part of the collection of the Galleria Nazionale d'Arte Antica ➡ 114. Most of the works were formerly owned by the Corsini family. They include a fine *John the Baptist* by Caravaggio and *Salome with the head of John the Baptist* by Guido Reni.

Villa Farnesina (57)

Via della Lungara 230 – 00165 Rome ☎ (06) 6886565

23, 65, 280 Lungotevere della Farnesina *Tues.–Sat. 9am–2pm; Sun. and public holidays 9am–1pm ● admission free*

This 'pleasure palace', whose gardens once ran down to the Tiber, was built by Baldassare Peruzzi (1509) to the orders of Agostino Chigi, a banker from Siena, who was also a man of letters and patron of the arts. He employed the greatest artists of his day, including the youthful Raphael. When owned by the Farnese family in 1580, it became known as the 'Farnesina'.

Not forgetting

■ **Janiculum Promenade (58)** *This promenade, laid out on the Janiculum hill at the end of the 19th century, offers commanding views of the city below.*

Lungotevere della Farnesina
Ponte Sisto
Tevere
Piazza G. G. Belli
Lungotevere Sanzio
Via della Lungara
Via dei Riari
Via Moroni
P.za Trilussa
Piazza Sonnino
V. d. Renella
Via S. Dorotea
Via Corsini
Via d. Scala
P. za De' Renzi
Via d. Lungaretta
Via S. Gallicano
PALAZZO TORLONIA
Via Garibaldi
Piazza S. Maria in Trast.
Via d. Fienaroli
V. d. Mattonato
Vicolo del Cedro
Via d. Paglia
P.za S. Calisto
Via S. Francesco a Ripa
V. d. Panieri
Via Luciano Manara
V. Del Grande
PARCO GIANICOLENSE
Via di Porta S. Pancrazio
Piazza S. Cosimato
Viale di Trastevere
V. Garibaldi
Passeggiata di Gianicolo
Via G. Mameli
V. L. Santini
Via E. Morosini
FONTANA D. ACQUA PAOLA
V. G. Sacchi
N
57
56
80
78
72
54
73
69
79
53
76
66
70
34
77
68
75
55
58
57
57
53
58

In the area

The Vatican is built on the site of the apostle Peter's tomb. Since the Lateran Treaty (February 11, 1929), it has been a sovereign state governed by the Pope. It is Europe's smallest state. ■ Where to stay ➡ 32 ■ Where to eat ➡ 54 ■ After dark ➡ 74 ■ Where to shop ➡ 152

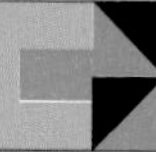

What to see

Piazza San Pietro (59)
00120 Città del Vaticano

The square, surrounded by majestic colonnades crowned with 140 statues of saints, is the masterpiece of Gian Lorenzo Bernini (1656–67). In the center stands the obelisk from Nero's Circus, set up here in 1586.

Basilica di San Pietro (60)
Piazza San Pietro – 00120 Città del Vaticano
☎ (06) 69883712 / 69884466

23, 34, 64 Via di Porta Castello ; 62 Via della Conciliazione ***Basilica Daily*** 7am–7pm ***Papal tombs Daily*** 7am–6pm ***Treasury Museum*** Daily 8am–6pm ● *no charge for admission to the basilica and papal tombs; Treasury Museum, dome 5,000 lire*

In 1506, wanting to affirm the power of the Holy See, Pope Julius II ordered the building of the largest church in Christendom. Work continued for a hundred and fifty years under a series of great architects: Bramante for the layout, Michelangelo for the dome, and Maderno for the nave and façade. The interior owes much to Bernini, who made the Catedra Petri (the bronze pulpit/reliquary)), the gigantic baldaccino (canopy protecting the throne of Saint Peter), and the tombs of popes Urban VIII and Alexander VIII. Be sure to see Michelangelo's moving Pietà, commissioned by Cardinal Bilhère de Lagraulas, undoubtedly the only sculpture signed by its author.

59

Musei Vaticani (61)

Viale Vaticano – 00120 Città del Vaticano ☎ (06) 69884947

23, 34, 64 Via di Porta Castello ; 62 Via della Conciliazione Mon.–Sat. 8.45am–4pm ● 15,000 lire

Housed in the sumptuous Vatican palaces, the museums are unique in the number and value of the works on display. The visitor has the opportunity to follow the history of art from Ancient Egypt to the 20th century. The crowning glories are the collections of antiquities, the Raphael Rooms, the Pinacoteca (art gallery), the Borgia Apartment, with frescos by Pinturicchio, and, last but not least, Michelangelo's dazzling Sistine Chapel.

Castel Sant'Angelo (62)

Lungotevere Castello 50 – 00193 Rome ☎ (06) 6875036

87, 492 V. Tiboniano; 280 Lungotevere Castello Daily 9am–7pm; Thurs., Fri., Sat. also 8.30–11.30pm; closed 2nd and 4th Tues. of month ● 8,000 lire

This building has had a checkered history. Originally an imperial tomb, it was later fortified, then became a nobleman's home and finally a papal residence. It is connected to St Peter's by a long corridor. The Ponte Sant'Angelo, by which it is approached, was embellished in 1667 with statues by Bernini depicting Christ's Passion.

Not forgetting

Palazzo Torlonia (63) Via della Conciliazione 3 – 00193 Rome
Attributed to Andrea Bregno, this elegant Renaissance building (not open to the public) was the setting, in the 19th century, for lavish parties thrown by the Torlonia family.

60 61 62

Hadrian's mausoleum, built in AD 123 in the gardens of Domitian, became the dynastic burial place of the Antonines. It was completed in AD 139, a year after the emperor's death.

In the area

The Tridente district gets its name from three streets fanning out from the Piazza del Popolo: the Via del Corso, with its monuments; the Via del Babuino, with its antique shops; and the Via di Ripetta, which led to the old river port. ■ Where to stay ➡ 22 ➡ 24 ■ Where to eat ➡ 48 ➡ 52

What to see

Piazza di Spagna (64)

The Spanish Steps are possibly the most delightful 'stage set' in the whole of Rome. The square gets its name from the city's first permanent embassy building, the Palazzo di Spagna, which is still the headquarters of Spain's embassy to the Holy See. Each year, the Pope comes to this square to celebrate the Immaculate Conception with a garland of flowers.

Trinità dei Monti (65)

Piazza della Trinità dei Monti 3 – 00187 Rome ☎ (06) 6794179

M A Spagna ◷ Daily 9am–12.30pm, 4–6pm ● admission free

This church was begun in 1502 at the request of the king of France, Louis XII. In the second chapel is one of the most celebrated frescos in Rome, Daniele da Volterra's *Deposition* (1541). Two centuries later, after many diplomatic wrangles, it was again with funding from the French royal coffers that Domenico Fontana built the majestic flight of steps, particularly attractive in spring when they are covered with azaleas. In the square below is the Barcaccia fountain (1629), thought to be the work of Bernini's father. It derives its name (leaky old boat) from its central feature.

Mausoleo di Augusto (66)

Piazza Augusto Imperatore – 00186 Rome

After defeating Antony and conquering Egypt, on his return to Rome in 29 BC Augustus built a grandiose mausoleum, inspired by that of Alexander the Great in Alexandria. It was intended to be a monument to his dynasty, and the first person buried there was his favorite nephew, Marcellus, who died in 23 BC. Neglected in the Middle Ages, transformed into a fortress by the Colonna family, used as a concert hall in the 19th century under the name of Augusteo, at one point it even served as a bullring.

Ara Pacis (67)

Lungotevere in Augusta – 00186 Rome ☎ (06) 68806848

M A Spagna ◷ Mon.–Sat. 9am–7pm; Sun. and public holidays 9am–1pm ● 3,750 lire; free on last Sunday of month

This altar, consecrated in 9 BC to celebrate the peace established by Augustus as a result of his victories in Gaul and Spain, is a magnificent monument to the art of the period. Its relief sculptures are the political propaganda of a regime based on legend, history and religion. The aim was to magnify Augustus and the Pax Romana. Fragments have been coming to light since the 16th century and the altar was reconstructed around 1930.

Not forgetting

■ **Santa Maria del Popolo (68)** Piazza del Popolo 12 – 00187 Rome ☎ (06) 3610836 *Behind its fine Renaissance façade, this church houses two masterpieces by Caravaggio,* The Crucifixion of Saint Peter and The Conversion of Saint Paul (1600–01). ■ **Via Condotti (69)** *A street renowned for* haute couture *and internationally famous jewelry businesses. Tucked away here is also Rome's oldest (1760) and for many years most prestigious café, the Caffè Greco.* ■ **Pincio (70)** *There is a fine view of the city from the promenade, laid out in the early 19th century in the gardens overlooking the Piazza del Popolo.*

After dark ➥ 84
Where to shop ➥ 144 ➥ 146

The Via Condotti, quintessence of Roman *haute couture*, was laid out in the 16th century to connect the Pincio with the banks of the Tiber.

65

64

67

69

The Villa Borghese, Rome's largest public park, is the archetypal pleasure garden. Its lawns are peppered with pavilions, statues and fountains, some of which date back to the Renaissance. The park was laid out by Cardinal Scipione Borghese, who also had the Casino built to house his collections.

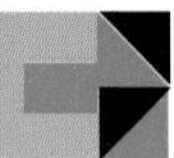

What to see

Museo e Galleria Borghese (71)

Piazza Scipione Borghese 5 – 00197 Rome ☎ (06) 8548577

52, 53, 910 Via Pinciana *Tues.–Sat. 9am–7pm; Sun. and public holidays 9am–1pm* ● *12,000 lire*

The Casino (little house), built around 1615, was enlarged and redecorated in the 18th century to provide a worthy setting for the family works of art, regarded as the 'queen of private collections'. Although the finest classical statues were sold to Napoleon by Prince Marcantonio, the museum still owns a good selection of Italian sculpture, for instance Bernini's *Rape of Proserpine* and *Apollo and Daphne*, and Canova's *Paolina Borghese*. The first-floor gallery houses a remarkable collection of Italian art, from the Renaissance to neoclassicism, including Raphael's *Deposition*, Antonello da Messina's *Portrait of a Man*, Caravaggio's *Young Man with a Basket of Fruit,* and Titian's *Sacred and Profane Love*. The building was reopened in June 1997, following restoration. There is also a minibus service linking the museum with the nearby Galleria d'Arte Moderna and the Villa Giulia.

Galleria Nazionale d'Arte Moderna (72)

Viale delle Belle Arti 131 – 00196 Rome ☎ (06) 322981 ➠ 3221579

19 Viale delle Belle Arti ; 926 Viale Buozzi *Tues.–Sat. 9am–7pm; Sun. and public holidays 9am–1pm* ● *8,000 lire*

The Palazzo delle Belle Arti (1911) houses one of the most interesting collections of 19th- and 20th-century Italian painting and sculpture. The neoclassical and romantic schools, history and 'metaphysical' painting, the Macchiaioli, the Futurists and all the main trends in 20th-century art are well represented, and space is also devoted to Italian regional and foreign movements. ★ The grand salon is dominated by Canova's group of *Hercules and Lichas*, a welcome addition to the Torlonia collection.

Museo Nazionale Etrusco di Villa Giulia (73)

Piazzale di Villa Giulia 9 – 00196 Rome ☎ (06) 3226571

19 Viale delle Belle Arti ; 926 Viale Buozzi *Tues.–Sat. 9am–7pm; Sun. and public holidays 9am–1.30pm* ● *8,000 lire*

Headquarters of the Etruscan Museum since 1889, the Villa Giulia was built by Vasari, Vignola and Ammanati (who created the splendid loggia enclosing the courtyard) as a summer residence for Pope Julius III (1551–5). The collections include priceless Etruscan and Faliscan artefacts, such as the golden tables of Pyrgi, the husband-and-wife sarcophagus from Cerveteri, some opulent jewelry, and polychrome terracotta ware from Portonaccio and Veio.

Not forgetting

■ **Piazza di Siena (74)** *Laid out at the end of the 18th century in imitation of a classical Roman circus, this square is the setting for the celebrated annual international riding competition.* ■ **Giardino del Lago (75)** *The waters of this small artificial lake, set in a neoclassical garden, reflect the columns of an Ionic temple dedicated to Asclepius. The Roman arch is by Luigi Canina (1827).*

73

73

71

73

74

In *The Rape of Proserpine*, the figure of Pluto is academic in style, while that of Proserpine shows Bernini's determination to achieve a more natural, life-like effect.

In the area

The Quirinal, which derives its name from the god Quirinus, was once the highest hill in Rome. A desirable residential area in Republican times, abandoned in the Middle Ages, it is now synonymous with politics: the Palazzo del Quirinale is the official residence of the Italian President.

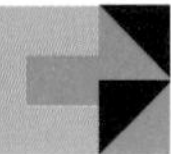

What to see

Sant'Andrea al Quirinale (76)
Via del Quirinale 26 – 00184 Rome ☎ (06) 4744801

M *A Barberini* ⏲ *Mon., Wed.–Sun. 10am–12 noon, 4–7pm* ● *admission free*

Gian Lorenzo Bernini regarded this church (1658) as his greatest achievement. Like the church of San Carlo, it is a perfect example of one of the two main styles developed by Roman baroque architects. Because of lack of space and the irregular shape of the site, Bernini adopted an ingenious oval plan which placed the worshipper at the very heart of the ceremony. The lighting brings out the beauty of the polychrome marble.

San Carlo alle Quattro Fontane (77)
Via del Quirinale 23 – 00184 Rome ☎ (06) 4883261

M *A Barberini* ⏲ *closed for restoration*

In tackling his first personal commission (1634), Borromini was faced with the same problem as had taxed his great rival, Bernini, with Sant'Andrea. He therefore designed an extraordinary elliptic cupola, achieving the illusion of height by making the coffering smaller toward the apex. The façade, with its interplay of concave and convex lines, was finished in 1685, some time after Borromini's death.

Galleria Nazionale d'Arte Antica (78)
Via delle Quattro Fontane 13 – 00184 Roma ☎ (06) 4814591

M *A Barberini* ⏲ *Tues.–Sat. 9am–1.30pm; Sun. and public holidays 9am–12.30pm* ● *8,000 lire*

This gallery was set up in 1895 and since 1949 has been housed in Palazzo Barberini (17th century). The few items from the original Barberini collections have been supplemented by works from other private collections, and paintings acquired by the Italian state. As a result the museum owns works by many of the great Italian and foreign masters of the 13th to 18th centuries. ★ In the reception room on the first floor, there is a magnificent ceiling painting by Pietro da Cortona (1632–6). The second floor, redecorated in the years 1750–70, provides an ideal setting for the 18th-century paintings.

Fontana di Trevi (79)
Piazza di Trevi – 00184 Rome

The most sparkling of Roman fountains was created for Pope Clement XII by Nicola Salvi. In the center stands Ocean, lording it over two sea horses being led by tritons. In the niches are statues of Abundance and Health. Tradition has it that a foreigner who throws a coin over his shoulder into the pool of the fountain will one day return to the Eternal City.

Not forgetting

■ **Via Veneto (80)** *The cafés, restaurants and hotels of this famous street are for ever associated with the luxurious lifestyle of the 'dolce vita'.*

■ **Galleria Colonna (81)** Via della Pilotta 17 and Piazza Santi Apostoli 53 – 00187 Rome ☎ (06) 6794362 *The opulent 18th-century rooms of the Palazzo Colonna house a fine collection of 14th–18th-century paintings and Roman statues.*

■ Where to stay ➥ 22 ➥ 34 ➥ 38 ■ After dark ➥ 74 ➥ 80 ➥ 84 ➥ 86

Borromini, the son of a Milanese architect and sculptor, came to Rome in 1621. He is the author of some of the city's most striking baroque buildings.

77

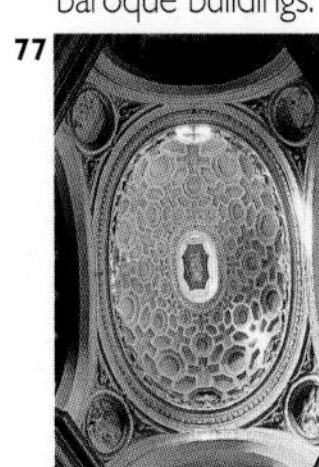

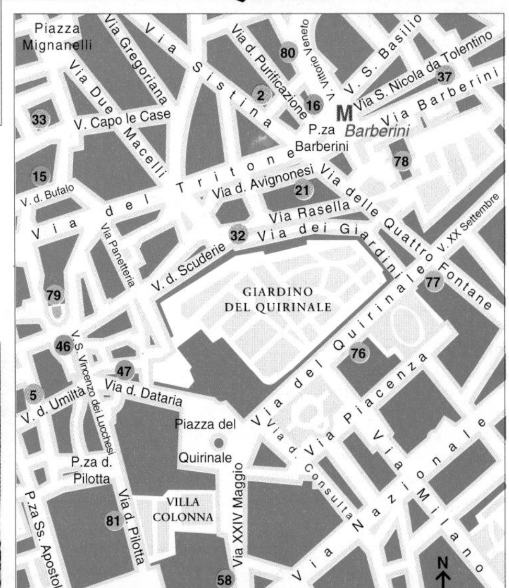

79

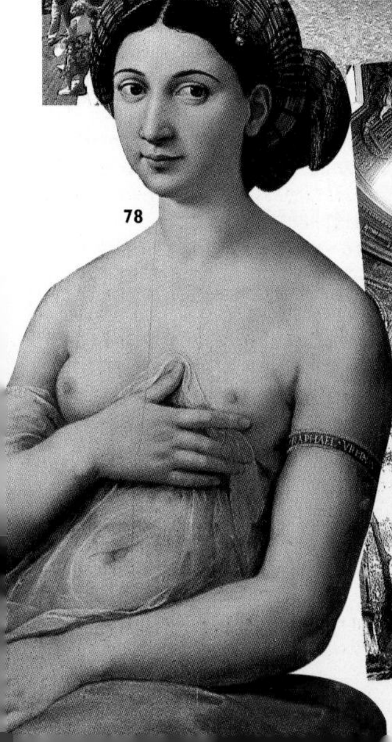

78

76

80

In the area

In this district, dignified classical monuments, baroque churches and grandiose *palazzi* exists side by side with twisting alleys, hidden passageways and tiny squares. A place of surprises. ■ Where to stay ➡ 34 ■ Where to eat ➡ 56 ■ After dark ➡ 74 ■ Where to shop ➡ 152 ➡ 156

What to see

San Luigi dei Francesi (82)

Piazza di San Luigi dei Francesi 5 – 00186 Rome ☎ (06) 688271

70, 115, 492 C. Rinascimento *Fri.–Wed. 7.30am–12.30pm, 3.30–7pm* ● *admission free*

The Contarelli chapel contains three masterpieces by Caravaggio (1597–1602): above the altar, *Saint Matthew and the Angel*; on the left, *The Calling of Saint Matthew*; on the right, *The Martyrdom of Saint Matthew*. ★ These works are representative of the painter's second period, when he began to experiment with violent contrasts of light and shade *(chiaroscuro)*.

Pantheon (83)

Piazza della Rotonda – 00186 Rome ☎ (06) 68300230

70, 115, 492 Corso del Rinascimento *Mon.–Sat. 9am–6.30pm; Sun. and public holidays 9am–1pm* ● *admission free*

The best preserved of all classical Roman buildings, because it was given to Pope Boniface IV by the Byzantine Emperor Phocas in AD 609 and converted to use as a church. The present building dates from the time of Hadrian, who replaced an earlier rectangular structure (25 BC). ★ The vast rotunda is crowned with a harmoniously proportioned coffered dome 142 ft in diameter – the largest masonry vault ever built. The 30-ft opening in the center is the only source of light. The niches are the last resting place of various artists, and of the Italian kings Victor-Emmanuel II and Umberto I.

Santa Maria sopra Minerva (84)

Piazza della Minerva – 00186 Rome ☎ (06) 6793926

60, 70, 492 Largo di Torre Argentina *Daily 7am–7pm* ● *admission free*

This church is so named because it stands on the site of a former temple dedicated to the goddess Minerva. Although rebuilt in 1280, it owes its present gothic features to an ill-conceived 19th-century attempt at restoration. Of special interest are the Carafa chapel (right transept), with frescos by Filippino Lippi, and a statue of Christ by Michelangelo (1519–20).

Galleria Doria-Pamphili (85)

Piazza del Collegio Romano 2 – 00186 Rome ☎ (06) 6797323

60, 492, 710 Via del Plebiscito *Fri.–Wed. 10am–5pm* ● *12,000 lire*

This private gallery houses the collections of the Aldobrandini, Pamphili and Doria-Pamphili families (successive owners of the *palazzo*). On display are some 400 works by Italian and foreign masters: Parmigianino, Titian, Caravaggio, Annibale Carracci, Velázquez and Claude Lorrain. It is also possible to visit the luxuriously furnished private apartments.

Not forgetting

■ **Palazzo della Sapienza (86)** Corso del Rinascimento 40 – 00186 Rome ☎ (06) 6864987 *In the courtyard stands the church of Sant'Ivo, by Borromini (1642–50), famous for the strange pinnacle crowning the lantern.* ■ **Sant'Ignazio (87)** Piazza di Sant'Ignazio – 00186 Rome ☎ (06) 6794560 *This church boasts a remarkable* trompe-l'œil *cupola, by Father Andrea Pozzo, a master of perspective.*

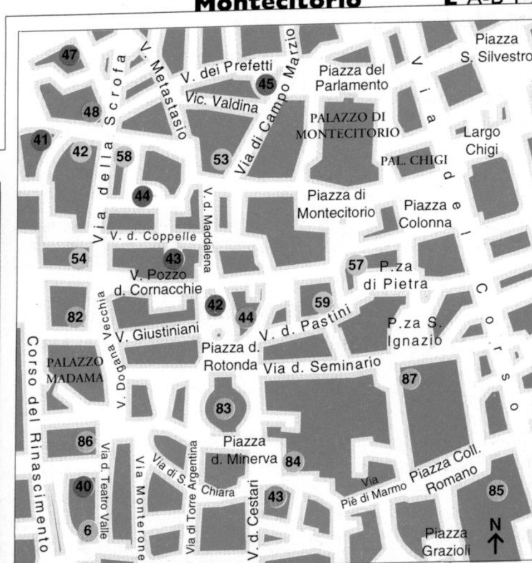
Piazza S. Silvestro
V. dei Prefetti
Piazza del Parlamento
V. Metastasio
Vic. Valdina
Via di Campo Marzio
PALAZZO DI MONTECITORIO
Largo Chigi
PAL. CHIGI
Via della Scrofa
Piazza di Montecitorio
Piazza Colonna
V. d. Maddalena
V. d. Coppelle
V. Pozzo d. Cornacchie
P.za di Pietra
Via del Corso
V. d. Pastini
P.za S. Ignazio
V. Giustiniani
Piazza d. Rotonda
Via d. Seminario
V. Dogana Vecchia
PALAZZO MADAMA
Corso del Rinascimento
Piazza d. Minerva
Via d. Teatro Valle
Via Monterone
Via di S. Chiara
Via di Torre Argentina
V. d. Cestari
Via Piè di Marmo
Piazza Coll. Romano
Piazza Grazioli
N
47
45
48
41
42
58
53
44
54
43
57
82
42
44
59
87
83
86
84
40
43
85
6

86

85

84

83

82

In the area
Closed to traffic, the Piazza Navona with its exuberant fountains is a jewel of baroque urban planning, a place to linger and get a feel for the Roman way of life. There are also fine Renaissance palaces in the area.
■ Where to stay ➥ 34 ➥ 36 ■ Where to eat ➥ 52 ➥ 58 ➥ 62

What to see

Piazza Navona (88)

70, 87, 115, 492, 628 Corso del Rinascimento

This square, adhering to the ground plan of Domitian's stadium (AD 81–96), is a good illustration of the continuity of Roman town planning. It also owes much to papal influence. Shortly after his election, in 1644, Pope Innocent X decided to embellish it to give his own palace a more impressive setting. He called on the great masters of baroque design, Bernini and Borromini, to remodel the Palazzo Pamphili, rebuild Sant'Agnese in Agone and construct the colossal Fontana dei Fiumi, symbolizing the four parts of the world: the Danube (Europe), the Nile (Africa), the Ganges (Asia) and the Rio de la Plata (America).

Palazzo della Cancelleria (89)
Piazza della Cancelleria – 00186 Rome

Although we do not know the identity of the architect of this elegant Renaissance palace (not open to the public) built for Cardinal Raffaele Riario, it is agreed that Bramante decorated the courtyard. In the time of Pope Paul III, in 1546, Vasari painted the frescos of the main reception room, claiming to have completed the work in a hundred days. As the headquarters of the Cancelleria, the department responsible for drawing up papal documents, the palace enjoys the same extraterritorial status as the Vatican.

Palazzo Farnese (90)
Piazza Farnese – 00186 Rome

46, 62, 64 Corso Vittorio Emanuele II ; 23, 65, 280 Lungotevere dei Tebaldi

Begun in 1510 by Antonio da Sangallo, Palazzo Farnese was completed by Michelangelo, who designed the second floor, the cornice and the two upper orders in the courtyard. The plans became a great deal more ambitious after Cardinal Farnese's election to the papacy, as Paul III, in 1534. The building now houses the French Embassy and is not open to the general public.

Palazzo e Galleria Spada (91)
Piazza Capo di Ferro 3 – 00186 Rome ☎ (06) 6861158

44, 65, 75 Via Arenula *Tues.–Sat. 9am–7pm; Sun. and public holidays 9am–1pm* ● *4,000 lire*

The stucco statues in the niches represent the great men of classical Rome (facing the square) and mythological deities (facing into the courtyard). ★ The palace is famous for the amazing perspective effect created by Borromini (1653), whose colonnaded gallery appears four times longer than it really is. Since 1927 the building has housed the Council of State. It is also home to the Galleria Spada, which owns a fine collection of 17th-century works.

Not forgetting
■ **Palazzo Massimo (92)** Corso Vittorio Emanuele II 141 – 00186 Rome *Palazzo Massimo alle Colonne was built in the mannerist style by Baldassare Peruzzi (1532–6). The façade is frescoed in grisaille. Not open to the public.* ■ **Museo Barracco (93)** Corso Vittorio Emanuele II 168 – 00186 Rome ☎ (06) 68806848 *An intimate collection of Egyptian, Assyrian, Etruscan, Roman and Greek sculptures.*

After dark ➥ 78 ➥ 80 ➥ 82 ➥ 84
Where to shop ➥ 154 ➥ 158 ➥ 162

93

89

88

88

90

In the area

In 1555, Pope Paul IV set up a Jewish ghetto in the Sant'Angelo district. Not until 1848 were the walls finally pulled down. The appearance of this district is compounded of Roman remains, aristocratic *palazzi* and fine churches, rubbing shoulders with kosher shops, *trattorie*, and

What to see

Teatro di Marcello (94)

Palazzo Orsini, Via di Monte Savello 30 – 00186 Rome

57, 81, 94, 628, 713 Via del Teatro di Marcello

The Emperor Augustus dedicated this imposing building to his nephew and heir designate, Marcellus, who died prematurely. Like many classical buildings, the theater was fortified in the Middle Ages. In the 16th century the Savelli family commissioned Baldassare Peruzzi to build the *palazzo* which now forms the upper floors. It was later remodeled by the Orsini, who lived there in the 18th century. The buildings surrounding the theater were demolished in 1926.

Portico di Ottavia (95)

Via del Portico d'Ottavia – 00186 Rome

The Corinthian columns which now form the portico of the church of Sant'Angelo in Pescheria were once part of a temple enclosure. Built originally in 146 BC, the portico was restored in the time of Augustus, who dedicated it to his sister, Octavia. The church takes its name (in Pescheria), from the fish market held on the forecourt in the Middle Ages.

Piazza Mattei (96)

44, 56, 181, 710 Via Arenula

This square provides a worthy setting for the splendid Fontana delle Tartarughe (tortoises), designed in 1581–4 by Giacomo della Porta and adorned with bronze sculptures by Taddeo Landini. In the 15th century, the square was practically taken over by the Mattei family, who erected a number of *palazzi* named after their feudal possessions. By far the most magnificent is the Palazzo Mattei di Giove, begun by Maderno in 1598. An extraordinary collection of antique marbles is on display in the courtyard (access at n° 32 Via Caetani).

Isola Tiberina (97)

23, 717 Lungotevere de' Cenci ; 774, 780 Lungotevere degli Anguillara

According to legend, this island in the Tiber is shaped like the boat used by Æsculapius, god of medicine, whom the Romans brought from Epidaurus, in Greece, to cure an outbreak of plague. Joined to the main embankment by the Ponte Fabricio (62 BC), the island still has a medical vocation, since it is occupied almost entirely by the Fatebenefratelli hospital. ★ Of special interest is the baroque decoration of the church of San Giovanni Calibita and, at the extreme southeast of the island, the remains of the Ponte Rotto, Rome's first stone bridge (181–179 BC), which collapsed in the 16th century.

Not forgetting

■ **Santa Maria in Campitelli (98)** Piazza di Campitelli - 00186 Rome ☎ (06) 68803978 *This late baroque church, designed by Carlo Rinaldi (1662), stands in one of Rome's most attractive lesser-known squares.* ■ **Mostra Permanente della Comunità Israelitica (99)** Lungotevere de' Cenci - 00186 Rome ☎ (06) 6875051 *Housed in the new synagogue, this Jewish museum features prints, silverware and liturgical vestments.*

craftsmen's workshops.
■ Where to stay ➥ 36
■ Where to eat ➥ 60 ➥ 64
■ After dark ➥ 84

96

95

94

99

97

Further afield

Savories from Palestrina

Feast your eyes on festoons of smoked sausages and charcuterie hanging from the beams. A paradise for lovers of such delicacies as *guanciale* (salted cheek of pig), *prosciutti* (hams) and *lonza* (loin of pork).

Macelleria suina di Bruno Cilia
Viale Ungheria 20
☎ *(06) 9537893*

Sweets from Frascati

Frascati produces some mouthwatering sweets: *ciambelle, biscotti, torroncini, pasticceria mignon* and *crostate di ricotta.*

Milletti *Via San Francesco d'Assisi 42*
☎ *(06) 9417373*
Purificato *Piazza del Mercato 4*
☎ *(06) 9420282*

How about a gelato?

Sorbets (*sorbetti*) and ice-creams (*gelati*), with more than forty flavors to choose from. Try the inimitable *gelato stracciatella* with whipped cream and chocolate chips. In fine weather you can enjoy your ice-cream on the terrace of the belvedere, overlooking Rome on one side and the Villa Aldobrandini, jewel of the Castelli Romani, on the other.
Bar Gelateria Belvedere *Piazza Roma 1, Frascati ☎ (06) 9424986*

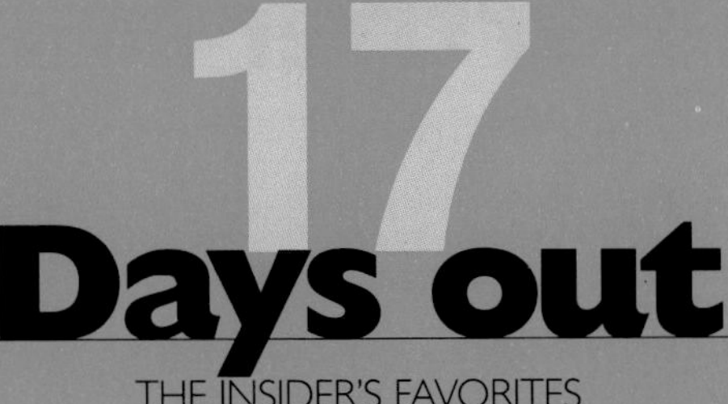

17 Days out

THE INSIDER'S FAVORITES

Sporting activities for the more adventurous

Try sailing from the beaches of Ostia.
Circolo Nautico Skipper Club
Via delle Orcadi, Lido di Ostia
☎ (06) 5646516
Circolo Velico Ostia Lido
Belvedere Carosio, Lido di Ostia
☎ (06) 5670282
Circolo Nautico Capitano Achab
Via degli Atlantici 26, Lido di Ostia
☎ (06) 56338060

Go rowing or canoeing on the Tiber, in the very heart of Rome.
Mariner Canoa Club
Passeggiata del Giappone, Roma EUR
☎ (06) 5913731
Go horse-riding in the pinewood (*pineta*) at Castelfusano.
Centro Ippico la Pineta
Via del Circuito 68, Castelfusano (between Ostia Antica and Lido di Ostia)
☎ (06) 50930096

INDEX BY TYPE

The area around the Eternal City, the Roman *campagna*, has many places to visit, reflecting its varied history: the archeological sites of Ostia (as well as the famous beaches of the Lido) and Hadrian's villa; the medieval towns of Palestrina, Tarquinia and Frascati; and the EUR, where Mussolini staged his universal exhibition in celebration of the Roman heritage.

Further afield

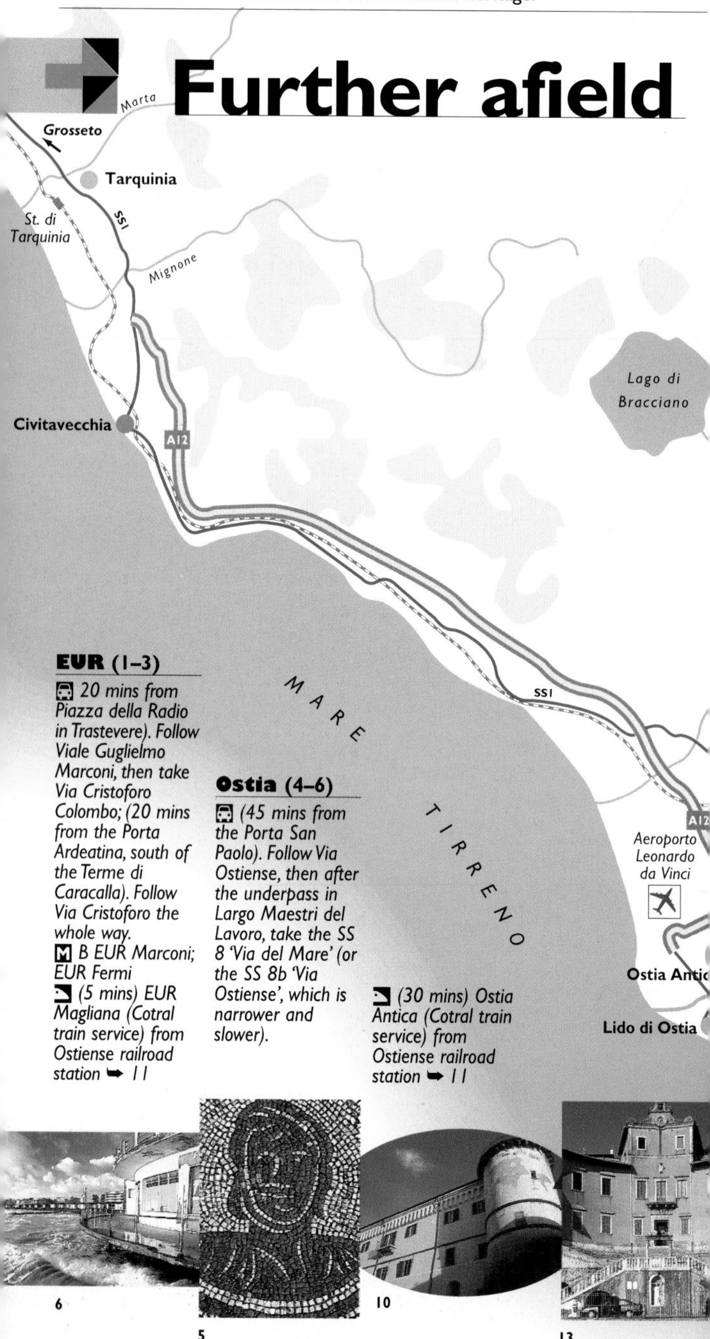

EUR (1–3)

(20 mins from Piazza della Radio in Trastevere). Follow Viale Guglielmo Marconi, then take Via Cristoforo Colombo; (20 mins from the Porta Ardeatina, south of the Terme di Caracalla). Follow Via Cristoforo the whole way.

M B EUR Marconi; EUR Fermi

(5 mins) EUR Magliana (Cotral train service) from Ostiense railroad station ➡ 11

Ostia (4–6)

(45 mins from the Porta San Paolo). Follow Via Ostiense, then after the underpass in Largo Maestri del Lavoro, take the SS 8 'Via del Mare' (or the SS 8b 'Via Ostiense', which is narrower and slower).

(30 mins) Ostia Antica (Cotral train service) from Ostiense railroad station ➡ 11

6

5

10

13

Frascati (7–10)

(c. 35 mins from the Porta San Giovanni). Follow Via Appia Nuova as far as the Piazza dei Rei roundabout, then turn left into Largo and Via Vercelli; then take Via Tuscolana; after the GRA (orbital road), take the SS 215 'Tuscolana'.

(c. 30 mins). Direct Cotral bus service.

(c. 35 mins). From Termini central railroad station ➡ 10, Via Ciampino

Palestrina (11–13)

(c. 40 mins from the Porta San Giovanni). Follow Via La Spezia as far as Piazza del Pigneto, turn right into Via Casilina, which after the GRA (orbital road) becomes the SS 6 'Casilina'; at San Cesareo, turn left onto the SS 155 toward Palestrina. For a more scenic drive (50 mins), take the SS 16 'Prenestina' from Porta Maggiore.

(c. 60 mins). Direct Cotral bus service.

Villa Adriana (14)

(c. 40 mins from Porta Maggiore). Take Viale dello Scalo S. Lorenzo toward the Circonvallazione Tiburtina (outer boulevard); then the A24 Rome–L'Aquila road, Tivoli exit; follow the SS 636 toward Tivoli, then turn right onto the SS 5 'Tiburtina'; after 1 mile, turn right towards the Villa Adriana.

A Cotral bus (M B), service leaves every hour from Rebibbia.

(c. 40 mins). From Termini central railroad station ➡ 10, or from Tiburtina station.

Tarquinia (15–17)

(c. 60 mins from Piazza della Radio). Follow Via Oderisi da Gubbio as far as Via Magliana heading toward the international airport; take the A12 on the Magliana viaduct; when the autostrada ends, take the SS 1 'Aurelia' for the last 3 miles to Tarquinia.

(c. 2 hrs 20 mins). Cotral bus service, change at Civitavecchia.

(c. 1 hour). From Termini central railroad station ➡ 10, Via Civitavecchia

14

15

14

Wanting to celebrate the 20th anniversary of the March on Rome with a universal exhibition (Esposizione Universale di Roma/EUR), in 1942 Mussolini ordered this monumental complex of buildings, which was intended to be the focal point of a new suburb. In 1951, after the disruption of the war years, the plans were revised and the EUR became an administrative center.

Further afield

Palazzo della Civiltà del Lavoro (1)

Quadrato della Concordia – V.le della Civiltà del Lavoro – 00144 Rome

M *B EUR Fermi*

Built between 1938 and 1943 to plans by Giovanni Guerini, Ernesto Bruno La Paluda and Mario Romano, this palace celebrating the virtues of hard work is undoubtedly the most characteristic feature of the EUR complex. The rhythmic pattern of the arcades is reminiscent of the amphitheaters of imperial times, such as the Colosseum ➥ 100. Continuing the classical theme, the four sculpted groups of the monumental staircase are modeled on the Dioscuri. The statues at ground-floor level are symbolic of the arts and other fields of human endeavor.

Palazzo delle Scienze (2)

Piazza Marconi 14 – 00144 Rome

M *B EUR Fermi* ***Museo Nazionale Preistorico Etnografico "Luigi Pigorini"*** *Piazza Marconi 14 – 00144 Rome ☎ (06) 549521 ⌚ Tues.–Fri. 9am–2pm; Sat. 9am–7pm; Sun. and public holidays 9am–1pm ● 8,000 lire* ***Museo dell'Alto Medioevo*** *Viale Lincoln 3 – 00144 Rome ☎ (06) 5925806 ⌚ Tues.–Sat. 9am–2pm; Sun. and public holidays 9am–1pm ● 4,000 lire*

This is the home of two major institutions: the 'Luigi Pignorini' museum of prehistory and ethnography and a museum devoted to medieval civilization. The first houses a collection of artefacts found in Italy and items from other continents. The second, inaugurated in 1967, displays ceramics, grave goods and jewelry dating from the 6th to 10th centuries, which were formerly kept in the Museo Nazionale Romano ➥ 102.
★ On the second floor there is a fascinating collection of aerial photographs of Italy's main archeological sites and natural phenomena.

Museo della Civiltà Romana (3)

Piazza Agnelli 10 – 00144 Rome ☎ (06) 5926041

M *B EUR Fermi ⌚ Tues.–Sat. 9am–6.30pm; Sun. and public holidays 9am–1.30pm ● 5,000 lire*

The two symmetrical buildings housing the museum of Roman civilization were donated to the city by Giovanni Agnelli, chairman of FIAT, after whom the square is named. Maps, plans, plaster casts and models spread over fifty-nine rooms illustrate the various aspects of Roman civilization and its pervading influence. The highlights are the plaster casts, made in 1860 on the orders of Napoleon III, of the reliefs of Trajan's column, and an impressive model of Rome by Italo Gismondi (2,152 square feet, the biggest ever made), reconstructing the city as it was in the time of Constantine (4th century).

Not forgetting

■ **Il Fungo** Piazza Pakistan 1 – 00144 Rome ☎ (06) 5921980 *Installed in a former water tower dominating the EUR, this restaurant has a stunning view. Classic cuisine with the emphasis on fish.* ■ **Shangri-La Corsetti** Viale Algeria 141 – 00144 Rome ☎ (06) 5916441 *Good service in a pleasant setting. Room with open fire, veranda doors opening onto the garden. The menu includes some specifically Roman dishes. Homemade confectionery and a good wine list.*

1

2

The building which epitomizes the EUR is the Palazzo della Civiltà del Lavoro, nicknamed the 'square Colosseum'.

3

3

3

Founded in the 4th century BC as a naval base at the time of Rome's struggle against Carthage, Ostia (from the Latin *ostium*, meaning river mouth) became Rome's main port of supply. It began to decline in the 4th century AD, when Constantine withdrew its privileges in favor of the artificial port of Portus Romae. What finally killed it were the incursions of Saracen raiders in

Further afield

Ostia Antica (4)

In 830, Pope Gregory IV founded a town to the northeast of the present excavations, on the site of a late-classical necropolis where Santa Aurea is buried. It is dominated by a fortress built by Baccio Pontelli (1485–6) for Cardinal Giuliano della Rovere, the future Pope Julius II (only the keep dates from the time of Martin V, 1417–31). Other buildings of note are the church of Santa Aurea, raised over the tomb of the martyr, and the bishop's palace, Palazzo Vescovile, which has frescos by Baldassare Peruzzi.

Scavi di Ostia Antica (5)

V.le dei Romagnoli 717 – 00119 Ostia Antica (RM) ☎ (06) 56358099

Museo Ostiense and excavations *summer: Tues., Wed., Sun. 9am–7pm; Thurs.–Sat. 9am–7pm, 8.30–11.30pm/winter: Tues.–Sun. 9am–4pm* ● *8,000 lire*

From the main gate, the Porta Romana, the *decumanus maximus* (main east-west street) leads to the Baths of Neptune, featuring the first mosaics with figurative motifs in black and white. Behind the theater, built by Agrippa, is the Piazzale delle Corporazioni, where the offices of navigation and trading companies, and the guilds involved in the fitting out and supply of ships, were housed under the surrounding portico. Their activities are depicted in the scenes on the magnificent pavement. The Via di Diana was a residential street, which in the time of Ostia's prosperity would have consisted of *insulae:* apartment blocks several stories high. On one side is a *thermopolium* (bistro) with a long counter of white marble. At the end of this street is the museum, which houses artefacts found on the site. At the crossing with the *cardo maximus* stands the forum and, on the northern side, the *capitolum*, with the city's main temple, dedicated to Jupiter, Juno and Minerva. Immediately opposite is the elegant temple of Rome and Augustus. Other buildings of interest are the luxurious House of Cupid and Psyche (4th century), the Serapeion, where the Egyptian god Serapis was worshipped, and the Baths of the Seven Wise Men, used by the inhabitants of the two adjacent *insulae.* ★ Beyond the Porta Marina, where a large suburb developed, is the oldest synagogue in the western world (1st century), discovered in 1961. Finally, beside the road connecting Ostia with Portus is the Isola Sacra necropolis, whose inscriptions and relief sculptures tell us a great deal about the social background of the people buried there.

Lido di Ostia (6)

Although the coastline has been spoilt by endless bathing establishments, and despite the pollution, the Romans still flock to these beaches of black sand, conveniently near to the city.

Not forgetting

■ **Le Bizze de "Il Tino"** Via dei Lucilii 19 – 00121 Lido di Ostia (RM) ☎ (06) 5622778 *An elegant restaurant, ideal for a candlelit dinner or lunch in the sunlit garden. Inventive, Mediterranean-style cuisine, strong on flavor. Excellent wine list.* ■ **L'Arcimboldo è al dente** Viale Vega 61 – 00121 Lido di Ostia (RM) ☎ (06) 5623329 *A paradise for pasta lovers. A hundred or so different varieties are on offer, classic and innovatory, earthy and sophisticated. The menu allows you to try several. Good choice of* hors-d'œuvres *and tempting array of homemade desserts.*

the 9th century. Rediscovered by archeologists in recent times, it represents a good example of a colony which grew rich on commerce.

4

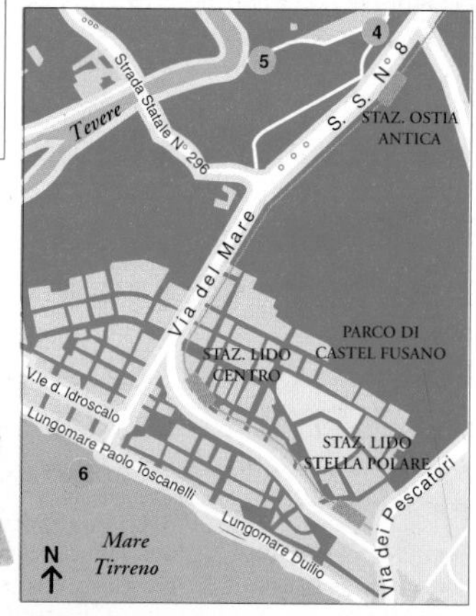

5

5

6

5

A summer resort of wealthy Roman citizens in classical times, and again in the Renaissance, the Castelli Romani area (18 miles southeast of the city) owes its name to thirteen small towns perched on the heights of the Alban Hills, which served as defensive strongholds (*castelli*) in the Middle Ages. Frascati, renowned for its golden-hued wine, is the largest

Further afield

Villa Aldobrandini (7)

Via G. Massaia 18 – 00044 Frascati (RM) ☎ (06) 9426887

Park *Mon.–Sat. 9am–1pm on application to the Azienda di Soggiorno*
● *admission free*

The villa's terraced gardens are an extravaganza of bubbling fountains and waterfalls, grottos, rockeries and statues, with a view over the countryside to the distant sea. Begun by Giacomo della Porta in 1598 for Cardinal Aldobrandini, nephew of Clement VIII, the villa was completed in 1604 by Carlo Maderno and Giovanni Fontana. The internal decoration is by the Zuccari and the school of Domenichino. Though it is the only one of Frascati's patrician residences open to the public, and that only in part, it is undoubtedly the most splendid. In the vicinity, it is also possible to visit the remains of two other 16th-century villas that were badly damaged in World War II: the Villa Lancellotti and the Villa Torloni, which was owned in turn by the Borghese, Colonna and Ludovisi families. Since 1954, its magnificent garden, with theatrical fountains by Carlo Maderno, has been Frascati's municipal park.

Cattedrale (8)

Piazza San Pietro – 00044 Frascati (RM) ☎ (06) 9420238

Daily 7am–noon, 3.30–7.30pm ● *admission free*

This church, dating from the 16th century, was given a baroque façade by Girolamo Fontana in 1697. The ground plan is that of a Greek cross. Inside there is a 12th-century wooden crucifix, a Madonna attributed to Domenichino and a painted wooden Virgin and Child of the 15th-century Roman school.

Chiesa del Gesù (9)

Piazza del Gesù – 00044 Frascati (RM) ☎ (06) 9417064

Mon.–Thurs., Sat. 7.15am–noon, 4–6.30pm; Sun. 9.15–noon, 4–6.30pm
● *admission free*

The attractive façade of this 17th-century church was designed by Pietro da Cortona. A strip of white marble in the paving leads to the ideal position from which to view the *trompe-l'œil* cupola. There is another frescoed cupola over the choir. The architectural settings for the altars are in fact two-dimensional. Some were painted by Andrea Pozza, a master of this kind of illusion.

Rocca (10)

Piazza Paolo III 10 – 00044 Frascati (RM) ☎ (06) 9420467

Now the bishop's palace, the medieval castle is decorated with fresco paintings, some in imitation of those found at Pompeii. The 15th-century courtyard is also worth visiting.

Not forgetting

■ **Cacciani** Via Diaz 15 – 00044 Frascati (RM) ☎ (06) 9420378 *This restaurant has been given a new lease of life: traditional dishes have been reinterpreted and new recipes introduced, with the accent on regional cuisine.*

and most frequently visited of these hilltop towns. Besides the view, it has some elegant patrician villas dating from the 16th century.

9

10

7

8

7

7

Built on the slopes of Monte Ginestro, Palestrina (Praeneste in classical times) controls a narrow pass. Already an important center in the 7th century BC, its fortunes ebbed and flowed before it reached a peak of prosperity in the 2nd century. A colossal construction program was undertaken at this time, including the spectacular sanctuary of the goddess

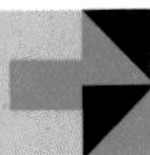

Further afield

Piazza Regina Margherita (11)

This square, in the center of the modern town, corresponds to the forum of ancient Praeneste. The cathedral stands on the site of a 4th/3rd-century BC temple, remains of which can still be seen outside the building and in the crypt. The north side of the forum was enclosed by a colonnade, part of which survives in the garden of the former seminary. There was also a basilica, flanked on the west by the 'cavern of fate' (a natural grotto which had been enlarged and decorated with a mosaic of sea creatures). To the east of the basilica was a great hall with an apse, a mosaic of the Nile and a black-marble statue (now kept in the Museo Archeologico), thought to have been a temple to Isis.

Santuario della Fortuna Primigenia (12)

Piazza della Cortina – Via del Tempio – 00036 Palestrina (RM)
☎ (06) 9538100

summer: Tues.–Sun. 9am–one hour before sunset / winter: Mon.–Sat. 9am–3.30pm; Sun. 9am–2pm ● 4,000 lire, ticket also valid for the Museo Archeologico

This extraordinary architectural complex, the largest built during the latter years of the Republic, was laid out on the hillside on six terraces. The lower terraces were supported by massive retaining walls. Above them a massive double ramp converged on a central stairway leading to the higher levels. On the terrace at the top of the staircase were two hemicycles of arcades with seats (exhedras) framed by a portico. The plinth in front of the right-hand exhedra is thought to have supported a statue of Fortune suckling Jupiter and Juno. Nearby is a well, into which a child would descend to bring up a tablet bearing an oracular message, which was read to the worshippers waiting for enlightenment. Farther up the hill was a terrace with niches framed by double columns, then a further terrace supporting the buildings of an upper temple. This terrace was screened on three sides by a portico consisting of a double row of columns, above which were ranged the tiered seats of a theater. Finally, the whole complex was crowned by a circular temple, built on the spot where honey was supposed to have dripped from an olive tree, indicating that Praeneste would become famous.

Palazzo Barberini e Museo Archeologico (13)

Piazza della Cortina – 00036 Palestrina (RM) ☎ (06) 9538100

summer: daily 9am–one hour before sunset / winter: Mon.–Sat. 9am–3.30pm; Sun. 9am–2pm ● 4,000 lire, ticket also valid for the Temple of Fortune

In 1630, the Colonna family sold Palestrina, which had suffered destruction several times under their lordship, to the Barberini. Ten years later, the palace which now houses the archeological museum was built around the ancient terraced theater. Its treasures include a large marble head which probably belonged to the statue of Fortune (late 2nd century BC), funerary artefacts from the local necropolis and ★ the magnificent mosaic of the Nile, depicting Egypt flooded by its waters. It dates from the 2nd century BC, when artists from Alexandria were working in Italy.

Not forgetting

■ **Il Palestrina** Via Toti 4 – 00036 Palestrina (RM) ☎ (06) 9534615 *Near the cathedral and main square, this restaurant serves affordable classic fare.*

Fortune. Praeneste began to decline in early Imperial times. In the Middle Ages the present town was rebuilt on the site of the former sanctuary.

11

13

13

13

13

13

Country retreat of the Emperor Hadrian (117–138), this villa complex stands on the slopes of the Tiburtini Hills, southwest of Tivoli. The beauty of the setting, extensive water gardens, variety of architecture and, last but not least, the sheer size of the place (300 acres) make it one of Italy's most fascinating archeological sites. A cultivated man and a great traveler, Hadrian,

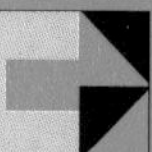

Further afield

Villa Adriana (14)

Via di Villa Adriana - 00019 Tivoli (RM) ☎ / ➟ (0774) 530203

Daily 9am–one hour before sunset ● *8,000 lire*

Built during the first ten years of Hadrian's reign, the complex consists of a series of pavilions skillfully integrated into the landscape (a model of the villa is on display in a modern building near the main entrance).

Pecile (A)

Consisting of a double portico enclosing a rectangular piazza with a garden and a swimming pool, this feature was inspired by the Stoa Poikile in Athens. Originally it was covered, and between the two rows of columns was a high central wall. It was laid out so that visitors could walk in the cool of the northern corridor in summer and in the more sheltered southern corridor in winter. There was also a fitness trail! The western part of the complex is built over an amazing substructure, the Cento Caramelle (hundred candies), which probably housed the staff.

Terme (B)

There were separate but adjacent bath houses for men and women. The fact that they were so near the Cento Caramelle suggests that they were for the use of the staff.

Canopo (C)

Situated in a valley, the Canopus is a long lake surrounded by a colonnade. Halfway along the western bank, the columns give way to caryatids, four of which are copies of those of the Erechtheion (one of the temples on the Acropolis in Athens) and two represent satyrs. The lake terminates at the northern end in a nymphaeum, which may have been used as an alfresco dining area in summer. It used to be thought that this complex was based on the Egyptian town of Canopus, connected to Alexandria by a canal and renowned for its temple of

C

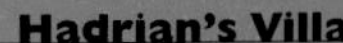

who himself drew up the plans, also wanted to be reminded of the wonders of his far-flung empire.

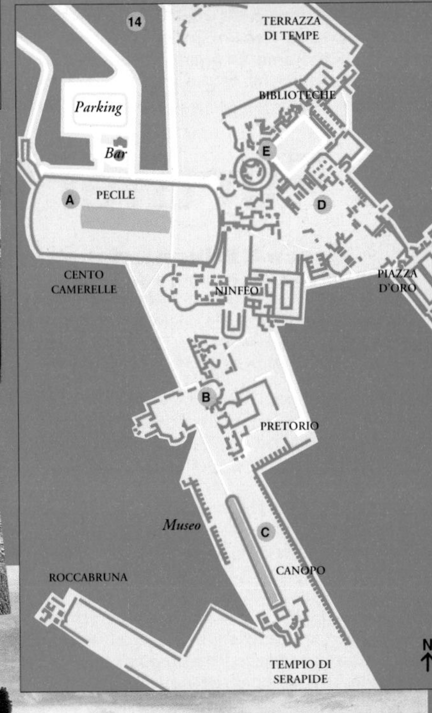

E

D

A

Serapis (identified with the nymphaeum). A more recent theory is that the lake represents the Mediterranean (hence the copies of celebrated statues evoking Greece and Asia Minor), while the architectural feature at the far end is suggestive of Egypt.

Palazzo Imperiale (D)

The palace consisted of three complexes of rooms, used for official functions and as a residence, each arranged around a courtyard: the libraries courtyard, the peristyle and the golden piazza. The most luxurious part of the villa was to the south of this piazza. The central room, open to the sky, was octagonal in shape, its sides alternately concave and convex. At one end was a large semi-circular nymphaeum, from each niche of which flowed a spring. This area was undoubtedly used as a *triclinium* (summer dining room).

Teatro marittimo (E)

Inappropriately named the maritime theater, this feature was a place of study and relaxation. It consisted of a miniature villa, built on an island. The island was surrounded by a canal and a portico and could be reached by two swing bridges.

C

The Etruscan city and the remains of its temple, the Ara della Regina, lie to the west of the medieval Tarquinia we know today. Little remains of one of the most powerful cities of Etruria, a religious center and the birthplace of Tarquin, king of Rome. Of greater interest nowadays is the necropolis, situated on another hill to the southeast, and the archeological museum,

Further afield

Museo Nazionale Tarquiniense (15)

Palazzo Vitelleschi, Corso Vittorio Emanuele – 01016 Tarquinia (VT) ☎ / ➟ (0766) 856036

Museum *Tues.–Sat. 9am–7pm ● 8,000 lire* ***Etruscan necropolis*** *group visits with museum guide (until 6pm)*

Museum The national museum is housed in the splendid old palace (1436–9) of the Vitelleschi, under whom Corneto (as it was then known) experienced its period of greatest prosperity. Sarcophagi, memorials, capitals and other architectural remains stand in rows in the arcaded courtyard. On the first floor, the exhibition includes the wonderful winged horses (late 4th to early 3rd century BC) from the Ara della Regina, and many funerary artefacts. As well as items from the Villanovan (Iron Age) and Roman periods, there are objects from the golden age of Etruscan civilization (7th–5th centuries BC): gold and bronze jewelry, and Greek vases which bear witness to Etruria's vast network of commercial contacts. Displayed on the second floor, which still has fragments of its painted 15th-century décor, are frescos removed from tombs in the necropolis. The museum also has a section devoted to medieval and modern art. **Etruscan necropolis** The museum organizes guided tours of the necropolis (taxis wait in Piazza Cavour for visitors unable to get there by car). The origin of the Etruscans is obscure. The classical writers are agreed that they were great builders, but little remains of their cities, and they have left little written evidence of their activities. It is the cities of their dead that have survived the centuries. Their tombs bear an extraordinary testimony to their religion, the development of their art and architecture, and their daily life. ★ The most striking feature of the tombs at Tarquinia are their mural paintings: the best of their kind to have survived from the pre-Roman world. Only a few of the *hypogea* are open to the public: the tombs of the Lionesses, the Leopards, the Augurs, the Orca, the Bulls and the Baron.

Santa Maria di Castello (16)

Piazza Castello – 01016 Tarquinia (VT) ☎ (0766) 864292

apply to the Società tarquinese d'arte e storia ☎ (0766) 858194 ● admission free

This church (1121–1208) is the most attractive of Tarquinia's medieval buildings. Tucked away in the oldest part of the town, it has an elegant, sober façade in three sections. The two-arched windows and doorway, and the flooring of the interior, are good examples of Cosmati marble work. Other interesting features are the octagonal baptismal fonts and the pulpit dating from 1209.

Palazzo Comunale (17)

Piazza Matteotti – 01016 Tarquinia (VT) ☎ (0766) 8491

Originally built in the 11th century, the town hall with its baroque façade is part of the rather theatrical Piazza Matteotti. Looking through the arches under the staircase, it is possible to make out the original Romanesque windows at the rear of the building.

Not forgetting

■ **Bersagliere** Via B. Croce 2 – 01016 Tarquinia (VT) ☎ (0766) 856047 *Lazio-region and fish specialties at reasonable prices, on the fringe of the old town center.*

housing one of the richest collections of Etruscan artefacts.

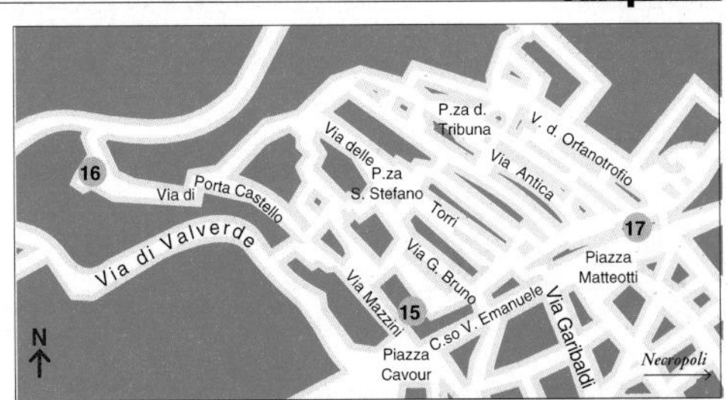

16

17

17

15

15

Where to shop

Open on Sundays

Department store

La Rinascente *Via del Corso (Tridente)*
☎ (06) 6797691 ⌚ 11am–7.30pm

Provisions

Riposati *Via delle Muratte 8 (Trevi)*
☎ (06) 6792866 ⌚ 7am–9pm

Photography

Vergerio *Piazza della Rotonda 66 (Pantheon)*
☎ (06) 6789913 ⌚ 9am–8pm

Books and newspapers

Libreria Internazionale *Via Tomacelli 144 (mausoleo d'Augusto) ☎ (06) 68808160*
⌚ 10.30am–1pm, 5–8pm

Larger sizes

If you are not exactly sylph-like, we can recommend a boutique in the Tuscalano district for elegant casual clothes. Brands include Marina Rinaldi, Liolà and Domina:

Taglie grandi
largo Magna Grecia 19/a
☎ (06) 70476720
⌚ 9am–1pm. 3.30–7.30pm; closed Monday mornings

Italian ice creams

Rome has an abundance of excellent *gelaterie*. Any Roman worth his salt will know one which sells 'the best ice creams in Rome'. Our own choice is: ***Il Palazzo del Freddo***

Via Principe Eugenio 65-67
00100 Rome ☎ (06) 4464740
Oct.–Mar.: Tues.–Thurs 3–9pm, Fri., Sat. 3pm–midnight; Sun. and public holidays 10am–10pm / Apr.–Sept.: Tues.–Sat. 3pm–midnight; Sun. and public holidays 10am–10pm

79 Stores

THE INSIDER'S FAVORITES

INDEX BY TYPE

In the area

These busy streets are popular with locals and visitors. Trendy boutiques mix with specialized establishments of long standing which have withstood the ups and downs of fashion. ■ Where to stay ➥ 20 ➥ 38 ■ Where to eat ➥ 46 ■ What to see ➥ 102 ■ Where to shop ➥ 162

Where to shop

Metropoli rock (1)

Via Cavour 72 – 00184 Rome
☎ (06) 4880443 ➟ (06) 485553

M *A, B Termini* ***Music*** 🕒 *Mon.–Sat. 9am–1pm, 4–8pm* 💳

An amazing choice of 45 and 33 rpm recordings (more than 300,000 in stock), CDs, cassettes, videos and videoclips covering the entire history of sound recording and all musical genres. A store where amateur and professional music buffs will want to spend days at a time.

Bottega dell'Arte (2)

Via di Santa Maria Maggiore 172 – 00185 Rome ☎ (06) 4881021

M *B Cavour* ***Interior design*** 🕒 *Mon.–Fri. 9.30am–1pm, 3.30–7.30pm; Sat. 9.30am–1pm*

A paradise for budding potters, this boutique may come as a surprise to the uninitiated. Investigating the shelves, you will find a whole range of household articles (especially for the kitchen and bathroom) needing to be painted and fired in a kiln. With their bare white appearance and simple lines, they would go well in some settings, even in their unfinished state.

Bottega delle chiusure lampo (3)

Via Panisperna 226 – 00184 Rome ☎ (06) 4828461

M *B Cavour* ***Haberdashery*** 🕒 *Tues.–Fri. 9.30am–1pm, 4–7pm; Sat. 9.30am–1pm*

The invention of the zipper brought about a minor revolution. Miniscule or massive, metal or nylon, here you will find zippers for all familiar purposes (clothing, leather goods, furniture, camping and sailing), and every new use a fertile imagination can devise.

Il tesoro (4)

Via dei Serpenti 135/136 – 00184 Rome ☎ / ➟ (06) 4871927

M *B Cavour* ***Gadgets, perfume, jewelry*** 🕒 *Mon. 4–8pm; Tues.–Sat. 9.30am–1pm, 4–8pm* 💳

A veritable bazaar, selling knick-knacks, perfumes, costume jewelry, clothing and curios from all parts of the world. The multi-colored jumble of items is no doubt intended to appeal to the young, but an adult short of ideas might unearth the very thing he or she is looking for: an original gift.

Not forgetting

■ **Gombo (5)** Via Principe Amedeo 289 – 00185 Rome ☎ (06) 4462322 ➟ (06) 4464272 *A supermarket specializing in exotic produce and ingredients. Enjoy discovering new flavors or, if you come from exotic parts yourself, the taste of home.*

■ **Santini Giacomo (6)** Via di Santa Maria Maggiore – 00185 Rome ☎ (06) 4880934 *Shoes for all the family – extravagant, strange and plain wacky.* ★ *Discounts of 50% and more all year round.*

STAZIONE TERMINI
Via Palermo
Via Milano
Via Cesare Balbo
Via Urbana
Via Cavour
V. Farini
Via Gioberti
Via Principe Amedeo
Via Filippo Turati
Via Giovanni Giolitti
Via Napoleone III
Via Carlo Alberto
Via Panisperna
Via Quattro Cantoni
Via Paolina
Via dell'Olmata
Via Merulana
Via Sforza
Via dei Serpenti
Via Giovanni Lanza
P.za S. Martino ai Monti
V. d. Statuto
L.go Venosta
Cavour M
Vittorio Emanuele M
N
1
2
3
4
5
6
7
8
9
10
41
45
46
47
59
78

3

4

4

2

1

In the area

Outwardly, the old working-class district of San Lorenzo has changed little over the years. But it has taken on a Bohemian air under the influence of its growing student population. The university is just around the corner. Rome's answer to the Boulevard Saint-Michel or Greenwich Village.

Where to shop

Said (7)

Via Tiburtina 135 – 00185 Rome
☎ (06) 4469204 ➠ (06) 4468210

11, 71 Via Tiburtina ; 492 Via dei Ramni ***Confectionery*** *Mon. 4–7.30pm; Tues.–Sat. 9am–1pm, 4–7.30pm*

This establishment is renowned for its sugared almonds, nougat, chocolate and other sweetmeats. People with a sweet tooth have been coming here for generations. ★ For baptisms, first communions, weddings and other special occasions, they make up gift boxes to suit every pocket.

Disfunzioni musicali (8)

Via degli Etruschi 4 – 00185 Rome
☎ (06) 4461984 ➠ (06) 4451704

11, 71 Via Tiburtina ; 492 Via dei Ramni ***Music*** *Daily 10.30am–7.30pm*

100,000 recordings in stock, featuring rock, funk, heavy metal, rap and experimental genres. ★ A further 50,000 titles are available secondhand, as special offers or otherwise discounted. Every kind of music is represented, except classical. You may well unearth the album you have been looking for to complete your collection. A must for music lovers passing through Rome.

Acquavetro (9)

Via degli Equi 26 – 00185 Rome ☎ (06) 44700951

11, 71 Via Tiburtina ; 492 Via dei Ramni ***Crafts, jewelry*** *Mon.–Sat. 9am–1pm, 3–7pm*

This workshop specializes in making large stained-glass windows, but also manufactures some attractive *bijou* items: earrings, pins, rings and pendants.

Macondo (10)

Via dei Latini 10 – 00185 Rome ☎ (06) 4460435

11, 71 Via Tiburtina ; 492 Via dei Ramni ***Jewelry*** *Mon.–Fri. 9.30am–1pm, 4.30–7.30pm; Sat. 9.30am–1pm*

A craft workshop specializing in the manufacture of handmade objects and items of jewelry following the latest fashion trends of the young. ★ Customers can also have items made to their own specification by bringing along a sketch.

Not forgetting

■ **Ottica Castri (11)** Via dei Salentini 22/24 – 00185 Rome ☎ (06) 4453636 ➠ (06) 4462845 *Vast selection of prescription- and sun-glasses ★ ready and waiting within an hour of your placing your order. Good value.*
■ **Bidonville (12)** Via dei Volsci 5 – 00185 Rome ☎ not on the telephone. *Store dealing in secondhand clothing, toys, recordings and old books, which can be purchased cheaply or traded for similar goods.*

Where to eat ➥ 52

10

10

9

7

In the area

The area around Piazza del Popolo has something for everyone, from foreign visitors to young people from the city's outer suburbs. Of course, you cannot splash out every day, but window-shopping is still great fun.

■ Where to stay ➡ 24 ■ Where to eat ➡ 48 ➡ 52

Where to shop

Buccone (13)

Via di Ripetta 19 – 00186 Rome ☎ / ➡ (06) 3612154

M A Flaminio ***Delicatessen, wines and spirits*** *Daily 9am–8.30pm*

This Roman institution jealously guards its original décor and its reputation for quality. ★ When aperitif time comes round, it becomes a *rendezvous* where customers swap gossip over a glass of wine. As well as an amazing range of high-class grocery products, Buccone is justly reputed for its spirits and wine cellar, where great foreign vintages and all Italy's wine-growing regions are gloriously represented.

Nia (14)

Via Vittoria 48 – 00187 Rome
☎ (06) 6795198 ➡ (06) 3222090

M A Flaminio ***Women's ready-to-wear clothing*** *Mon. 3–7pm; Tues.–Sat. 10am–2pm, 3–7pm*

This boutique will appeal to women whose idea of elegance includes discretion and refinement, but who do not want to appear unfashionable. A good place to know, if you are looking for basic items: suits, overcoats, dresses. There is also a good choice of accessories.

Tad (15)

Via di San Giacomo 5 – 00187 Rome
☎ (06) 36001679 ➡ (06) 36001809

M A Flaminio ***Interior design, furniture*** *Mon. 3–7pm, Tues.–Sat. 10am–7pm*

If you are the sort of person who looks to the future without despising the past, and if you are thinking of revolutionizing your home, this could be the place for you. Here you will find a studiedly casual mixture of avant-garde creations and items of antique furniture from goodness knows where. Old and new are combined with great sensitivity.

Bacillario (16)

Via Laurina 41/43 – 00187 Rome ☎ / ➡ (06) 36001828

M A Flaminio ***Children's ready-to-wear*** *Mon.–Sat. 9.30am–1.30pm, 3.30–7.30pm*

Very young children will undoubtedly feel more at home in this small boutique than in many megastores. A miniature paradise for those who have decided they want to look more 'way-out' than their friends. Items include shoes so bizarre they would look more at home in a modern art gallery!

Not forgetting

■ **B.B.K. (17)** Via della Frezza 60 – 00186 Rome ☎ (06) 3244259 ➡ (06) 3243668 *Furniture, utilitarian items and accessories for bathroom, kitchen and bedroom. Originality is the rule.*

■ **Bomba (18)** Via dell'Oca 39 – 00186 Rome ☎ / ➡ (06) 3612881 *Clothes for women who believe that elegance is a matter of proportion and good taste. There is also a children's department.*

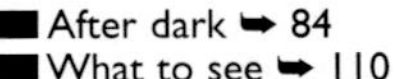

After dark ➥ 84
What to see ➥ 110

14

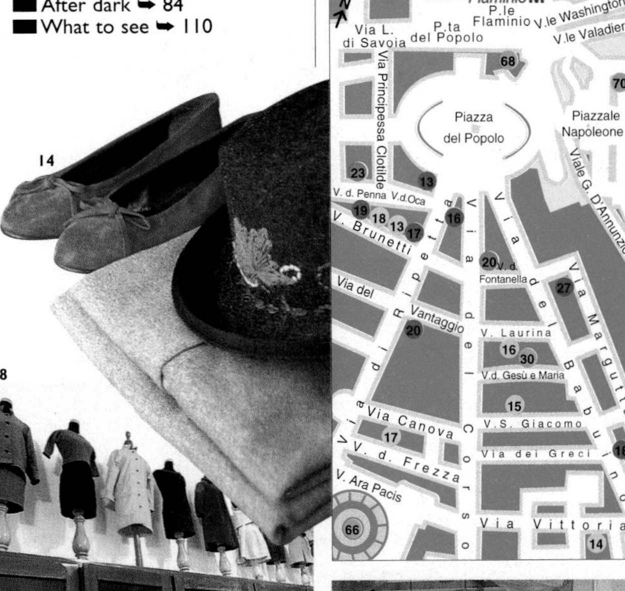

18

15

18

13

In the area

The small grid of streets between Via del Corso and Piazza di Spagna ➡ 110. is a showcase for much of the Italian haute couture industry. A delight for the eyes, likely to lead into temptation. ■ Where to stay ➡ 22 ➡ 24 ■ Where to eat ➡ 48 ➡ 52 ■ After dark ➡ 86

Where to shop

Boutique Miss V (19)

Via Bocca di Leone 15 – 00187 Rome
☎ (06) 6795862 ➡ (06) 6739394

M *A Spagna* ***Haute couture*** *Mon. 3–7pm; Tues.–Sat. 10am–7pm*

In 1959, Valentino Garavani opened his workshop in nearby Piazza Mignanelli, where Sophia Loren, Audrey Hepburn and Jackie Kennedy came to order some of the most daring evening dresses of recent decades. The décor of this 1960s boutique is a reminder of his dazzling début. Everything is redolent of elegance and dashing creativity. In his hands, even a pair of jeans is transformed into formal attire.

Fendi (20)

Via Borgognona 38 – 00187 Rome ☎ (06) 6797641 ➡ (06) 69940808

M *A Spagna* ***Haute couture*** *Mon. 2–7.30pm; Tues.–Sat. 10am–7.30pm*

In New York, the street would already have been renamed in honor of the Fendi sisters. But this is Rome. The merits of this legendary duo are nevertheless beyond dispute. Originally furriers, they won their place in the demanding world of women's fashions when they branched out into ready-to-wear clothing and accessories. They were assisted to some extent by Karl Lagerfeld, who designed their double 'F' motif. You will be charmed by the setting, the warm welcome and the beauty of the products themselves.

Laura Biagiotti (21)

Via Borgognona 43 – 00187 Rome ☎ (06) 6791205 ➡ (06) 6795040

M *A Spagna* ***Haute couture*** *Mon. 3.30–7.30pm; Tues.–Sat. 10am–1.30pm, 3.30–7.30pm*

The great Roman designer has gradually won her place in the sun with a very personal style of clothing featuring bright colors and garments suited to every occasion. Here she exhibits her creations in the setting they deserve. The friendly, competent staff will help you find just the right garment or accessory, if what you are looking for is not on display.

Not forgetting

■ **Domus (22)** Via Belsiana 52 – 00187 Rome ☎ (06) 6789083 ➡ (06) 6783122 *Wide selection of women's shoes. The accent is on the quality of the leather and the finishing. A fairly classic style, though some models are more contemporary.* ■ **Energie (23)** Via del Corso 407 – 00187 Rome ☎ (06) 6871165 *A megastore featuring loud music and bright lights, where younger customers can stock up on jeans, T-shirts and leather jackets. A combination of the useful and the frivolous.* ■ **Lilia Leoni (24)** Via Belsiana 86 – 00187 Rome ☎ (06) 6790514 ➡ (06) 6783210 *A collection of antique furniture, with the emphasis on things British and a country cottage style.* ■ **Alcozer (25)** Via delle Carrozze 48 – 00187 Rome ☎ / ➡ (06) 6791388 *A place of elegance and nostalgia. Fine jewelry inspired by the Belle Époque and the 1920s, and not excessively expensive.* ■ **Materozzoli (26)** Piazza di San Lorenzo in Lucina – 00186 Rome ☎ / ➡ (06) 6871456 *A range of mainly French and British perfumes, and sophisticated, unusual accessories.*

What to see ➥ 110

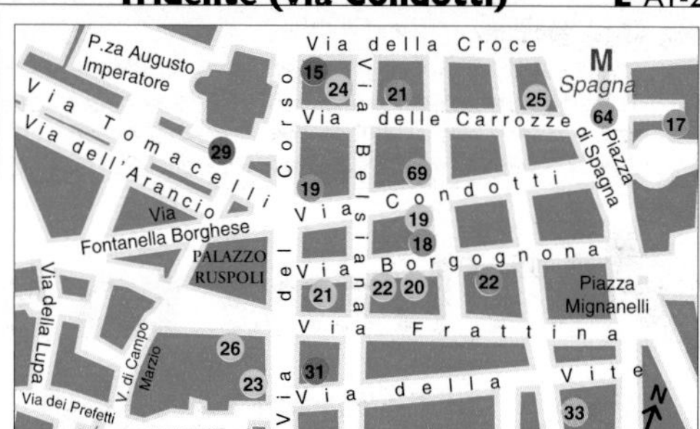

19

20

20

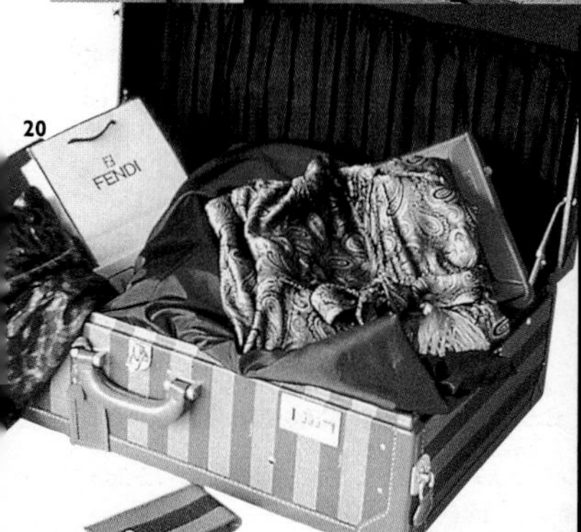

20

Skilled craftsmanship, things you want to touch: the Fendi sisters can look to the future confident in their mastery of styles of the past.

19

In the area

The prestigious Parioli district has managed to retain the tranquil atmosphere on which its reputation was based. Its serene character is reflected in its boutiques, where everything appears well laid out and orderly. A contrast with the feverish business community that is steadily invading its streets.

Where to shop

La Vecchia Marina (27)
Viale Buozzi 13 – 00197 Rome ☎ / ➠ (06) 8070422

52, 926 Viale Buozzi ***Antiques*** *Mon. 4–7.30pm; Tues.–Sat. 9.30am–1pm, 4–7.30pm*

Sailing enthusiasts will applaud the enterprise of the owners, who have combed the world in search of ships' furniture and maritime memorabilia. ★ Visit the extraordinary collection of old navigational instruments: compasses, sextants, chronometers, and so on.

Equitana (28)
Via Siacci 32 – 00197 Rome ☎ / ➠ (06) 8079831

919, 926 Via Siacci ***Sports equipment*** *Mon. 4–7.30pm; Tues.–Sat. 9am–1pm, 4–7.30pm*

Undoubtedly Rome's best-stocked store for lovers of equestrian sports. Riding habits, saddles, bridles and other accessories, all impeccably designed both functionally and esthetically.

Age d'Or (29)
Via Oxilia 6b/c – 00197 Rome ☎ (06) 8079609

3, 53, 168 Viale dei Parioli ***Ready-to-wear children's clothing*** *Mon. 4–8pm; Tues.–Sat. 9am–1pm, 4–8pm*

Mothers and grandmothers will not be able to resist the baby and toddler clothing on sale here. Casual garments for sports and leisure activities, more formal dresses and suits for special occasions. Attractive babywear and a wealth of new ideas.

Atmospheres (30)
Via Manfredi 4/a – 00197 Rome ☎ (06) 8078185

919, 926 Via Antonelli ***Antiques*** *Mon. 3.30–7.30pm; Tues.–Sat. 9.30am–1.30pm, 3.30–7.30pm*

An attractive antique shop crammed with small items of furniture, glassware, knick-knacks, English silverware and lamps in Liberty style (the Italian version of Art Nouveau). Reminiscent of a Paris or London antique dealer, a good place for a root around.

Not forgetting

■ **Giù & ga (31)** Viale dei Parioli 114 – 00197 Rome ☎ (06) 8075578 ➠ (06) 2412525 *A pleasant store selling designer seconds at tempting prices. Ready-to-wear men's and women's clothes, shoes, accessories and lingerie.*

■ **Righetto Sport (32)** Via Castellini 6 – 00197 Rome ☎ (06) 8078073 *A vast store selling clothing and accessories for all sporting activities, and leisure wear generally.*

■ **Jyp de fleures (33)** Via Mercalli 16 – 00197 Rome ☎ (06) 80687759 *Woolens for everyday wear and special occasions. Elegant, well-cut clothing with a nod to the current fashion.*

■ Where to stay ➥ 28 ■ Where to eat ➥ 50

27

28

29

30

In Parioli, one of Rome's most exclusive districts, children's tastes are taken very seriously.

29

In the area

Around the law courts and barracks of the Prati district, not far from the Vatican, a lively commercial complex of large stores and boutiques has grown up over the years. The main customers here are locals, attracted by the variety of goods on offer and a fair pricing policy.

Where to shop

New Old (34)
Via Marcantonio Colonna 12 – 00192 Rome ☎ / ➠ (06) 3214804

M *A Lepanto* ***Interior design, furniture*** *Mon. 4–8pm; Tues.–Sat. 9.30am–1.30pm, 4–8pm*

If this store had a motto, it would be 'satisfying the most contrary needs'. The established classics of every bride's list are unselfconsciously displayed alongside small items of furniture you will find nowhere else, silver trays, plastic tableware, stylish furniture and high-tech gadgets.

G. Giuliani marrons glacés (35)
Via Paolo Emilio 67 – 00192 Rome ☎ / ➠ (06) 3243548

M *A Ottaviano* ***Confectionery*** *Mon.–Sat. 8.30am–8pm; Sun. 9am–1pm*

Apparently so simple in comparison with the many more complex inventions of master confectioners, the *marrons glacés* of our youth still have the power to make the mouth water. Fresh, smooth, melt-in-the-mouth, the ones sold by Giuliani are quite irresistible.

Pergioco (36)
Via degli Scipioni 109/111 – 00192 Rome ☎ (06) 39737179

M *A Ottaviano* ***Toys*** *Mon. 3.30–7.30pm; Tues.–Sat. 9.30am–1pm, 3.30–7.30pm*

Entirely devoted to the concept of play, this store stocks Rome's widest range of video and electronic games. They also have a good selection of role-play games.

Atelier della cravatta (37)
Via Marcantonio Colonna 4 – 00192 Rome ☎ (06) 3214294

M *A Lepanto* ***Men's accessories*** *Mon. 3.30–7.30pm; Tues.–Sat. 9.30am–1pm, 3.30–7.30pm*

Plain, striped, floral, check... here you will not only find the necktie you need, but also make some unexpected discoveries, for instance ties with animal motifs. The textures are every bit as varied and interesting as the patterns.

Not forgetting

■ **Alexandra (38)** Via Paolo Emilio 19 – 00192 Rome ☎ (06) 3243311 ➠ (06) 3244926 *Women's shoes in a wide range of styles. What they have in common is that they are daring, if not provocative, often with a touch of humor.*
■ **Habitat (39)** Via Cola di Rienzo 197 – 00192 Rome ☎ (06) 3230136 ➠ (06) 3243126 *A wealth of ingenious ideas and solutions, spread over two floors. You may be inspired to reorganize your house from top to bottom.*
■ **Vestiastock (40)** Via Germanico 170/a – 00192 Rome ☎ / ➠ (06) 3224391 *Sales all the year round. Branded and unbranded clothing, formal and casual, for men, women and children. A rapid turnover of stock.*

After visiting the Vatican, call in at G. Giuliani's and let yourself be tempted by the *marrons glacés* (45,000 lire the kilo) he has been making so expertly for the last forty-five years. A mere venal sin!

In Rome you will find a wide range of craft products, which make welcome gifts. As well as articles from other parts of Italy, there is a long tradition of local craftsmanship. Silver is a Roman specialty. Worked into many different forms, it is believed to bring luck. Offering a present made of silver is a time-honored Roman custom.

Shopping

45
43
43

Italia Garipoli (41)

Borgo Vittorio 91/a – 00193 Rome ☎ (06) 68802196

🚌 *23, 64 Via di Porta Castello* ***Interior design*** 🕒 *Mon.–Fri. 10am–1pm, 2–7pm; Sat. 10am–1pm*

Ask in London, Brussels or Paris and they will tell you that Italian collectors are among the greatest connoisseurs and buyers of old embroidered linen. If proof were needed of the almost insatiable demand for these valuable household items, Italy still has many skilled seamstresses employed on quilts, towels and embroidered linen curtains. ★ This workshop also offers the unusual service of restoring old fabrics.

Bottega Mortet (42)

Via dei Portoghesi 18 – 00186 Rome ☎ / ➟ (06) 6861629

🚌 *119 Via della Scrofa; 87, 70 Via di Ripetta* ***Wrought-iron work*** 🕒 *Mon.–Fri. 9am–6pm*

In this workshop, hidden away in an aristocratic old residence, the art of metal working has been passed down from father to son for three generations. ★ You can buy or order skillfully crafted artefacts, or just enjoy watching them being made.

Fratelli Bertoni (43)

Piazza dei Quiriti 10 – 00192 Rome ☎ / ➟ (06) 3207199

Ⓜ *A Lepanto* ***Taxidermy, jewelry*** 🕒 *Mon. 4.30–7.30pm; Tues.–Sat. 10.30am–1pm, 4.30–7.30pm*

Representatives of a dying and controversial craft, the Bertoni brothers see their work as a celebration of nature. As well as hunting trophies, they sell collections of colorful butterflies and insects, tropical shells and coral – imaginatively arranged to create jewelry from nature.

The best boutiques can be found in the Piazza Cola di Rienzo.

Before leaving Rome, buy a special souvenir or item of value to show that, on the eve of the third millennium, the skills of the past are still alive and well.

Romana Stucchi (44)

Via Aurelia 181 – 00165 Rome ☎ (06) 39366542

46 Via Aurelia ***Interior design*** *Mon.–Fri. 9am–noon, 3.30–7.30pm*

One of the last survivors of many Roman workshops specializing in stucco work. On display you will find a profusion of cornices, consoles, ceiling roses, antique decorative features and floral ornaments, as well as low reliefs, capitals and columns. Some are very traditional; others novel variations on a neoclassical theme.

Laboratorio Ilaria Miani (45)

Via degli Orti d'Alibert 13/a – 00165 Rome ☎ / ➠ (06) 6861366

23, 41, 65 Lungotevere Gianicolense ***Interior design*** *Tues.–Sat. 10am–1pm, 3.30–7pm*

At the foot of the Gianicolo (Janiculum hill), in an unexpectedly tranquil setting, this workshop is devoted entirely to wood-carving. You can buy picture frames, from stock or made to order, as well as imaginative table lamps, book shelves, mirrors and footrests.

Annamaria Stirpe (46)

Via Pasubio 4 – 00195 Roma ☎ (06) 3201481 ➠ (06) 3244971

628, 926 Lungotevere delle Armi ***Interior design*** *Mon.–Fri. 8.30am–5pm*

This workshop is for those who are not totally satisfied by the well-known brands of household linen. Here they aspire to something more personal, something unique: the feminine touch of embroidered white curtains, the freshness of an immaculate sheet distinguished by a delicate design, the refinement of a towel marked with one's own monogram, the smooth whiteness of a richly embroidered tablecloth. ★ Articles can also be made to order.

In the area

The traffic-free Piazza Navona ➡ 118, with its wealth of historic monuments, is the square where the vibrancy of Roman life is most apparent. Souvenir shops abound in the labyrinth of streets around the square. ■ Where to stay ➡ 36 ■ Where to eat ➡ 56 ➡ 58 ➡ 62

Where to shop

In folio (47)

Corso V. Emanuele II 261/263 – 00186 Rome ☎ / ➡ (06) 6861446

62, 64 Corso Vittorio Emanuele II ***Interior design*** *Mon. 3.30–8pm; Tues.–Sat. 10am–8pm*

Good design is the factor common to all the goods displayed in this cheerful, well-lit store. Clocks and watches, pens, toasters, can-openers, soap dishes, each has that something extra which holds the attention, be it the material used, the simple, uncluttered style, or the unmistakable 1940s/1950s inspiration.

Berté (48)

Piazza Navona 108 – 00186 Rome ☎ (06) 6875011 ➡ (06) 68801068

62, 64 Corso Vittorio Emanuele II; 70, 87 Corso del Rinascimento ***Toys*** *Mon. 3.30–7.30pm; Tues.–Sat. 9.30am–1pm, 3.30–7.30pm*

While adults gaze in wonder on the monuments of Piazza Navona, children's eyes will light up at the tantalizing shop window displays. Berté's window advertises the magical world of toys and games. Inside, your little darlings can choose from a vast range of traditional toys, dolls, soft toys and the latest games.

Contemporanea (49)

Via dei Banchi Vecchi 143 – 00186 Rome ☎ / ➡ (06) 68804533

62, 64 Corso Vittorio Emanuele II ***Interior design*** *Mon. 4–8pm; Tues.–Sat. 10am–1pm, 4–8pm*

If you have exhausted the possibilities of antique dealers, secondhand shops and contemporary designers, try this workshop. The accent is on the theatrical, the baroque, the fantastic: not so much interior decoration as exuberant stage sets. Inventive furnishings to help you create your own unique environment.

Paola Vassarotti (50)

Vicolo della Cuccagna 12 – 00186 Rome ☎ / ➡ (06) 6893209

62, 64 Corso Vittorio Emanuele II ***Women's ready-to-wear clothing*** *Mon.–Sat. 11am–1pm, 4–8pm*

Woolens and other garments designed for comfort, elegant but without exaggeration, definitely not the sort of clothes you wear only once. And an attractive line of practical accessories you will love to have about you.

Not forgetting

■ **Stock market (51)** Via dei Banchi Vecchi 51/52 – 00186 Rome ☎ (06) 6864238 ➡ (06) 6832336 *Furniture, crockery, kitchen implements, watches: anything cheap with a touch of class finds its way to this store.*

■ **Sempreverde (52)** Via del Corallo 7 – 00186 Rome ☎ (06) 68801398 *An Eldorado for those who get a buzz from buying things secondhand. And you may well come away with a bargain.*

After dark ➥ 78 ➥ 80 ➥ 82
What to see ➥ 118

50

49

47

49

In the area

Around the Pantheon and the parliament building of Montecitorio, tourist and Roman, man-in-the-street and politician rub shoulders every day. The varied needs of so divergent a clientele are reflected in the stores of this interesting district. ■ Where to stay ➡ 34

Where to shop

Davide Cenci (53)

Via di Campo Marzio 1/7 – 00186 Rome
☎ (06) 6990681 ➡ (06) 6795900

56, 60, 175 Via del Corso ***Ready-to-wear clothing*** *Mon. 4–7pm, Tues.–Sat. 10am–7pm*

This outfitter has been clothing the well-dressed Roman for the last seventy-five years, in its own exclusive Davide Cenci creations and other famous labels. The store is old-fashioned in layout, with separate departments for each type of clothing and style: women's clothing, menswear, children's section, lingerie, woolens, city suits, sportswear, and so on.

La città del sole (54)

Via della Scrofa 65 – 00186 Rome ☎ (06) 68803805 ➡ (06) 6875404

70, 87 Corso del Rinascimento ***Toys*** *Mon. 3.30–7.30pm; Tues.–Sun. 10am–7.30pm*

Swimming against the tide, this store has no place for the cheap, plastic and tacky. Wood, canvas, cardboard and other natural materials predominate. As well as the wonderful toys, likely to touch the heart of the child in each of us, there is a vast range of educational and board games.

Agostini Arte Arredo (55)

Via del Clementino 106 – 00186 Rome
☎ (06) 6873632 ➡ (06) 3614391

70, 87 Via di Ripetta ***Antiques*** *Mon. 4–8pm; Tues.–Sat. 9.30am–1pm, 4–8pm* ***Cosmati Galleria Antiquaria*** *Via Vittoria Colonna 11 – 00193 Rome ☎ (06) 3611141*

A competently run, highly professional store, with rooms devoted to furniture, paintings, sculpture and bronzes of the different European schools, china and Oriental carpets.

Massimo Maria Melis (56)

Via dell'Orso 57 – 00186 Rome ☎ / ➡ (06) 6869188

70, 87 Via di Ripetta ***Jewelry*** *Mon. 3.30–7.30pm; Tues.–Sat. 9am–1pm, 3.30–7.30pm*

The jewelry created by goldsmith Massimo Maria Melis is quite unique. Like an alchemist with power over past and present, he combines antique materials (coins, pieces of glass or crystal) with precious metals to produce necklaces, bracelets, rings, brooches and earrings with an ambiguous, slightly disturbing quality.

Not forgetting

■ **Caleffi (57)** Via della Colonna Antonina 53 – 00186 Rome ☎ (06) 6793773 *Classic dresses, suits and overcoats.* ■ **Sirni (58)** Via della Stelletta 33 – 00186 Rome ☎ / ➡ (06) 68805248 *A furrier who welcomes suggestions from clients. Superb styling and painstaking workmanship.* ■ **Il sigillo (59)** Via della Guglia 69 – 00186 Rome ☎ / ➡ (06) 6789667 *Pens, writing paper, photograph albums, envelopes, visiting cards. All beautifully finished.*

Where to eat ➥ 56

54

56

53

55

In the area

The carefree, ironic spirit of the Campo de' Fiori is reflected in its retail businesses. There is a strong element of novelty, extravagance and provocation, qualities to appeal to the young, trendy intellectuals and people with maybe more money than sense! ■ Where to stay ➥ 36

Where to shop

Loco (60)

Via dei Baullari 22 – 00186 Rome ☎ (06) 68808216 ➟ (06) 8552942

62, 64 Corso Vittorio Emanuele II ***Shoes*** *Mon. 3.30–8.30pm; Tues.–Sat. 10.30am–8.30pm*

The place for unusual footwear. Here shoes come in daring combinations of colors and materials, and original styles with inventive heels and lacings.

Vacanze Romane (61)

Via degli Specchi 20 – 00186 Rome ☎ / ➟ (06) 6875672

44, 170, 710 Via Arenula ***Interior design*** *Tues.–Sat. 10am–1.30pm, 3.30–8pm*

Craft products from all five continents to get you out of your rut and broaden your horizons. Unusual, curious and sometimes amusing articles, to bring life, color and warmth to every corner of the house and garden.

Baullà (62)

Via dei Baullari 37 – 00186 Rome ☎ (06) 6867670

62, 64 Corso Vittorio Emanuele II ***Women's ready-to-wear clothing*** *Mon. 4–7.30pm; Tues.–Sat. 10am–1.30pm, 4–7.30pm*

The entrance lobby of an old building converted into a boutique: ★ a setting with definite sculptural qualities. The owners have adopted an original approach to feminine fashion, borrowing ideas from other parts of the world. The result is a very personal hybrid style.

Taba (63)

Piazza Campo de' Fiori 13 – 00186 Rome ☎ (06) 68806478

62, 64 Corso Vittorio Emanuele II ***Gadgets*** *winter: daily 10am–8pm; summer: daily 10am–midnight*

The attractive aspect of this boutique is the rainbow of bright, vivid colors that greet you from the shelves. It stocks an incredible variety of candles, costume jewelry and accessories, and many less useful items with no obvious function!

Not forgetting

■ **Planet (64)** Via dei Baullari 132 – 00186 Rome ☎ (06) 68801396 *Fashion wear for the young, especially those whose cultural reference is the UK and the USA. Some amazing shoes and no end of jeans.* ■ **Claudia Bleicher (65)** Vicolo del Bollo 6/7 – 00186 Rome ☎ (06) 68309111 ➟ (06) 6808282 *Locally made silver jewelry featuring semi-precious stones, and more exotic oriental jewelry.* ■ **Ibiz (66)** Via dei Chiavari 39 – 00186 Rome ☎ / ➟ (06) 68307297 *Craftsmen in leather, producing travel bags, purses, satchels, card wallets and pocketbooks, and some more unusual articles.* ★ *Goods made to order.* ■ **Arti e mestieri (67)** Via dei Cappellari 57 – 00186 Rome ☎ (06) 6832521 *This workshop restores and decorates old furniture. The display also includes some of its own iron, wooden and ceramic products.*

■ Where to eat ➥ 52 ➥ 58 ➥ 60 ■ After dark ➥ 80 ■ What to see ➥ 118 ■ Where to shop ➥ 162

60

60

63

3

61

62

61

In the area

Trastevere may have become a district of restaurants and night spots, but has not lost its credentials as a working-class stronghold. Tour its stores and workshops in the morning to discover its traditional good-natured character. ■ Where to eat ➡ 62 ➡ 64 ➡ 66

Where to shop

Drogheria Innocenzi (68)

Piazza di San Cosimato 66 – 00153 Rome ☎ (06) 5812725

44, 75, 170 Viale di Trastevere ***Specialized grocery store*** *Mon.–Wed, Fri., Sat. 7am–1.30pm, 4.30–7.30pm; Thurs. 4.30–7.30pm*

Those who dream of old-fashioned grocery stores with big sacks of dry goods, rice and flour standing in rows behind the counter will feel at home here. They can also stock up on specialties, Italian regional products and commodities from abroad, often not to be had for love nor money elsewhere. ★ Faced with so tempting a choice, the visitor is in danger of ending up with an overweight suitcase.

Modi e Materie (69)

Vicolo del Cinque 4 – 00153 Rome ☎ (06) 5885280

44, 75, 170 Viale di Trastevere ; 23, 65, 280 Lungotevere Sanzio ***Interior design, jewelry*** *Mon.–Sat. 10.30am–1pm, 5–8.30pm*

When traditional craftsmen adopt contemporary fashion without at the same time abandoning tried-and-tested values, the results can be surprising. Here natural materials, *papier mâché*, wood, fabrics and ceramics are fashioned, combined, colored and decorated with great creative freedom. Fernanda Retico will welcome you to view this exhibition of prototypes and finished articles, and her daughter will show you some exciting creations in the decorative art studio at n° 13. A visual delight, like visiting an art gallery.

AZI (70)

Via di San Francesco a Ripa 170 – 00153 Rome
☎ / ➡ (06) 5883303

44, 75, 170 Viale di Trastevere ***Interior design*** *Mon.–Sat. 9.30am–1.30 pm, 4–8pm; Sun. 4–8pm*

A vast range of household items with the accent on quality of design. Made of unpretentious materials, such as glass, terracotta and even tinplate, they tend to be unusual, curious and above all useful! ★ Here you can gather ideas for brightening up a dull corner of the house, or find an attractive and original present, without having to dig too deep into your pocket.

Not forgetting

■ **L'albero della vita (71)** Piazza in Piscinula 2/3 – 00153 Rome ☎ (06) 5809072 *A herbalist where health and beauty go hand in hand. Herbs and infusions, and body-care products made from natural ingredients.*
■ **Lattonieri (72)** Piazza de' Renzi 22 – 00153 Rome ☎ (06) 5806737 *Oil-and-vinegar stands, coffee pots, buckets, lanterns and other old-fashioned utensils made of tinplate. They are crafted by two brothers who will also be pleased to make you something to order if you let them have a sketch.*
■ **Il canestro (73)** Via di San Francesco a Ripa 106 – 00153 Rome ☎ (06) 5746287 *A pioneer in macrobiotic food. Still one of Rome's best-stocked retailers of natural and organic products.*

■ After dark ➥ 86 ■ What to see ➥ 98 ➥ 106

70

68

69

69

68

70

It is often said that if you really want to understand a town you must visit its markets. Whether they sell foodstuffs or a great range of goods, like the one at Porta Portese, Rome's markets reveal a double identity. On the one hand, the unmistakable cocky accent and gestures of the Roman working class; on the other, a Rome which, as capital of an empire and

Markets

75 77 74

Mercato di Campo de' Fiori (74)
Piazza Campo de' Fiori

62, 64 Corso Vittorio Emanuele II **Foodstuffs** *Mon.–Sat. 6am–2pm*

At first glance, there is a surprising number of people taking photographs. No doubt because it is difficult to resist such a feast of colors, shapes and contrasts. The second impression is the quality of the produce: fruit and early vegetables, pork products and other specialties. Maybe this explains the rather steep prices for what is after all a local market.

Mercato di Porta Portese (75)
Via di Porta Portese

23, 717, 780 Lungotevere di Ripa Grande ; 13, 170, 280, 719 Viale di Trastevere
Old clothes, secondhand goods, foodstuffs *Sun. 5am–2pm*

Every Sunday morning, the square is invaded by crowds of people who thread their way between stalls which stretch from the Porta Portese as far as the Piazza Ippolito Nievo, the Ponte Testaccio and the Piazzale della Radio. Several acres of new and secondhand merchandise, official and clandestine, local and exotic, real bargains and some awful old junk.

center of Christendom, is destined to embrace the whole world. Markets are held in many districts of the city. These are some of the most characteristic.

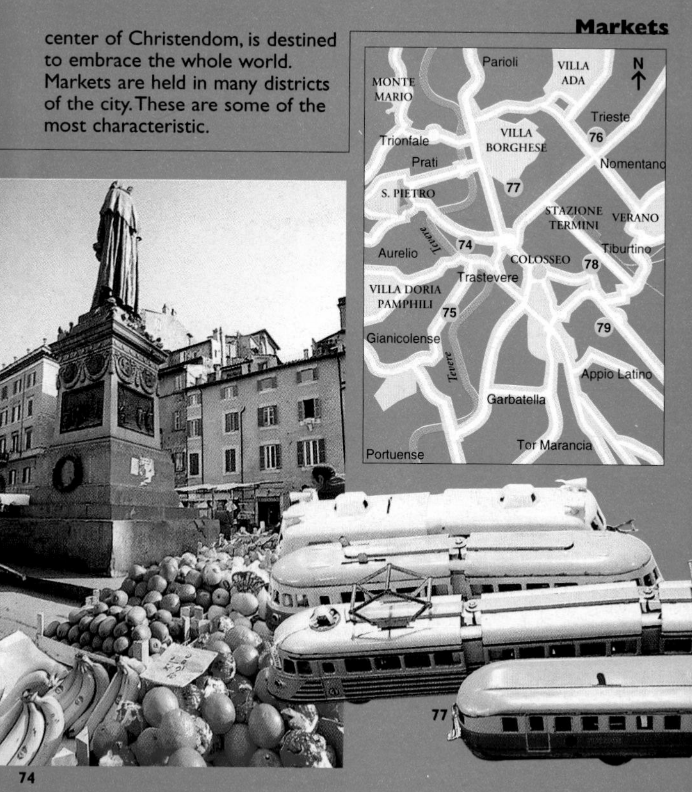

77

74

L'antico in Terrazza Peroni (76)

Via Mantova 24 (Autosilo) – 00198 Rome ☎ (06) 9067980

490, 495 Porta Pia **Secondhand goods** *3rd Sunday of the month 10am–8pm ● 2,500 lire*

More than fifty vendors set up their stalls on the top floor of this underground car park (*autosilo*) in the former Peroni brewery. Secondhand goods, articles ancient and modern, collectors' items.

Underground (77)

Via Crispi 96 (Parking Ludovisi) – 00187 Rome ☎ (06) 69940440

M *A Barberini* **Secondhand goods** *1st weekend of the month: Sat. 3–8pm; Sun. 10.30–7.30pm ● 2,500 lire*

A colorful meeting point for collectors and bargain hunters. Few of the vendors or purchasers are in the trade. They tend to be private individuals driven by their particular enthusiasm. ★ The section devoted to children and adolescents (young and not so young) is original and great fun. There they will find everything you can imagine – and many things you cannot – to complete even the most unusual collection.

Not forgetting

■ **Mercato di Piazza Vittorio Emanuele II (78)** *A popular foodstuffs market with an increasingly exotic flavor, where recent immigrants from many different sources mix with native-born Romans.* ■ **Mercato di Via Sannio (79)** *New and secondhand clothes, camping gear, car and motorcycle accessories: the Porta Portese market in miniature, but held every day. Better organized than its larger rival and very well stocked. You may find a bargain.*

Finding your way

The seven hills of Rome

Founded in the 7th century BC by Romulus on the Palatine, Rome gradually spread to the six neighboring hills, with new settlements growing up on the Capitoline, the Quirinal, the Viminal, the Esquiline, the Celian and the Aventine.

The city walls

The Aurelian Walls, built c. 275 BC, have always protected the heart of Rome, except in 1870, when the Piedmontese army gained possession of the city. Rome was then incorporated into the kingdom of Italy and eventually became the capital..

Street vocabulary

Borgo: suburb
Circonvallazione: outer boulevard
Fiume: river
Largo: square
Lungotevere: Tiber embankment
Piazza: square
Piazzale: esplanade
Ponte: bridge
Rione: district
Via: street
Viale: avenue
Vicolo: lane

10 Maps

INDEX OF THE DISTRICTS OF ROME

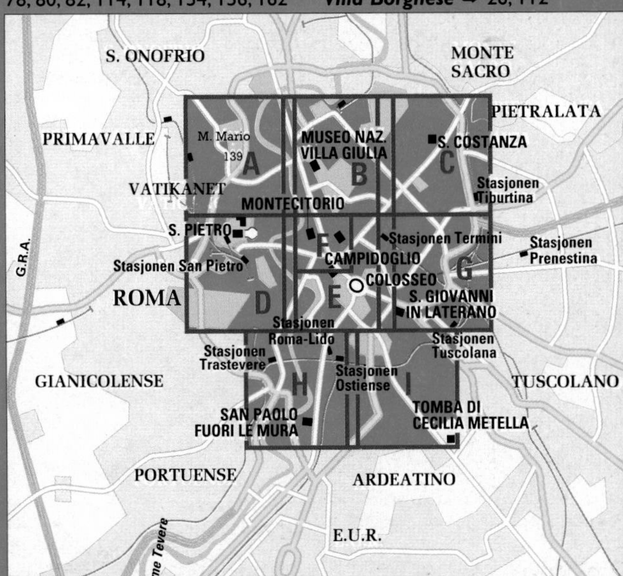

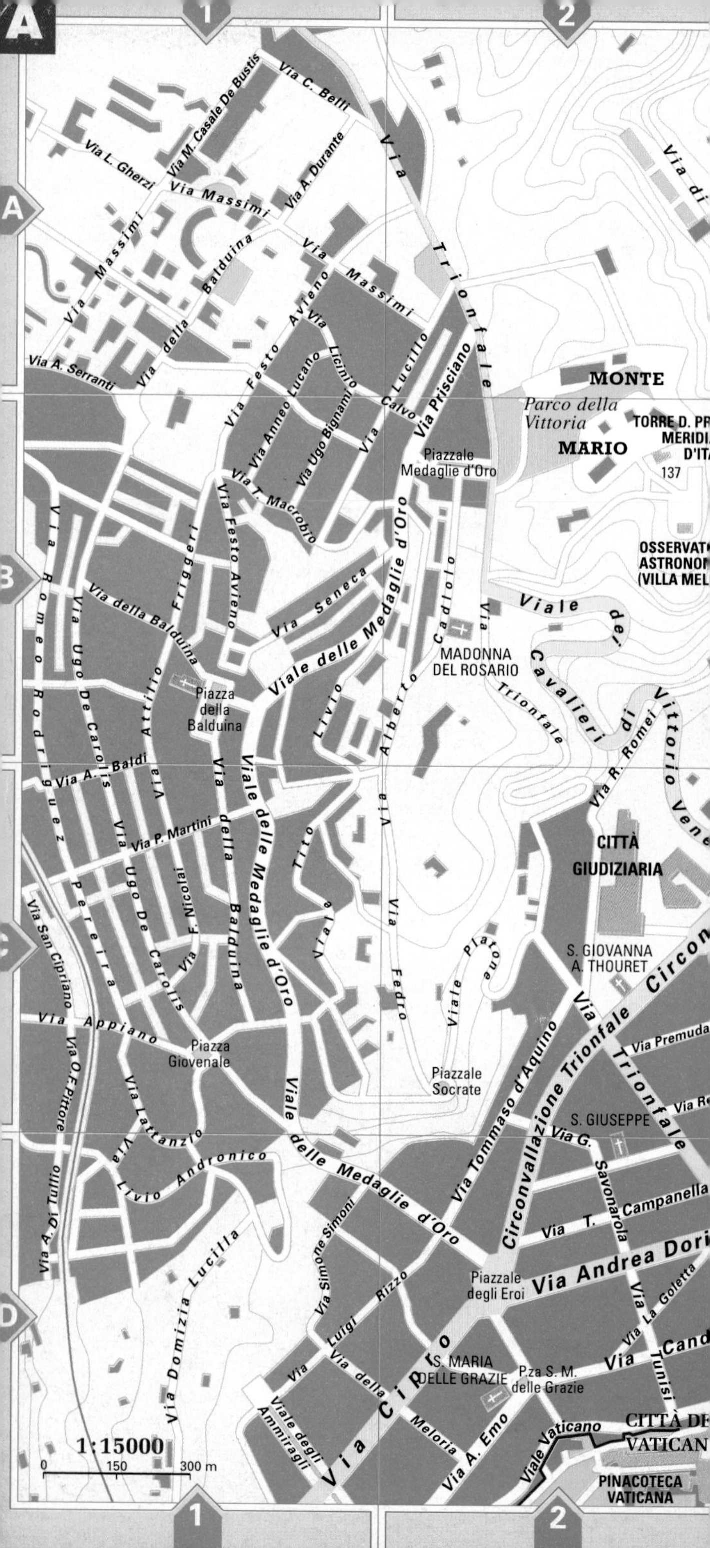
A
1
2
MONTE
MARIO
Parco della Vittoria
TORRE D. PR
MERIDI
D'IT
137
OSSERVAT
ASTRONOI
(VILLA MEL
Piazzale Medaglie d'Oro
MADONNA DEL ROSARIO
Piazza della Balduina
CITTÀ GIUDIZIARIA
S. GIOVANNA A. THOURET
Piazza Giovenale
Piazzale Socrate
S. GIUSEPPE
Piazzale degli Eroi
S. MARIA DELLE GRAZIE
P.za S. M. delle Grazie
CITTÀ DE
VATICAN
PINACOTECA VATICANA
Via C. Belli
Via M. Casale De Bustis
Via L. Gherzi
Via Massimi
Via A. Durante
Via Balduina
Via Trionfale
Via Aviena
Via Licinio
Via Lucilio
Via Calvo
Via Prisciano
Via Festo Avieno
Via Lucano
Via Anneo
Via Ugo Bignami
Via A. Serranti
Via della Balduina
Via T. Macrobio
Via Friggeri
Via Seneca
Viale delle Medaglie d'Oro
Via Cadlolo
Viale dei Cavalieri di Vittorio Vene
Via R. Romei
Via Alberto
Via Livio
Via Tito
Via Romeo Rodriguez
Via Ugo De Carolis
Via Attilio
Via A. Baldi
Via P. Martini
Via F. Nicolai
Via Pereira
Via San Cipriano
Via Appiano
Via O. F. Pittore
Via Lattanzio
Via Livio Andronico
Via A. Di Tullio
Via Domizia Lucilla
Via Fedro
Viale Platone
Via Tommaso d'Aquino
Circonvallazione Trionfale
Via Premuda
Via G. Savonarola
Via T. Campanella
Via Andrea Dori
Via Simone Simoni
Via Luigi Rizzo
Via La Goletta
Via Tunisi
Via Cand
Via Cipro
Via della Meloria
Viale degli Ammiragli
Via A. Emo
Viale Vaticano
1:15000
0 150 300 m
B
C
D

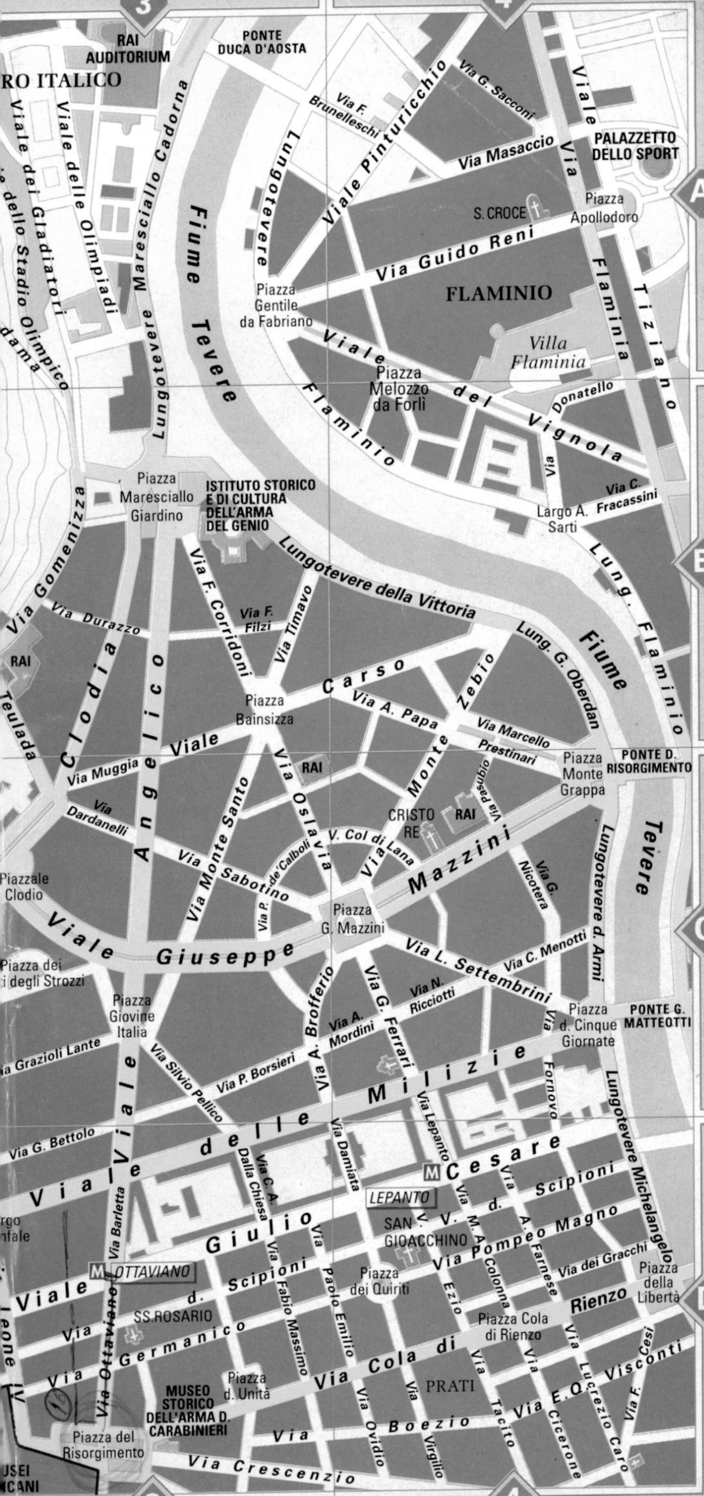
3
4
A
B
C
D
RAI AUDITORIUM
PONTE DUCA D'AOSTA
RO ITALICO
Viale delle Olimpiadi
Viale dei Gladiatori
dello Stadio Olimpico
Maresciallo Cadorna
Lungotevere
Fiume Tevere
Via F. Brunelleschi
Viale Pinturicchio
Via G. Sacconi
Viale
Via Masaccio
PALAZZETTO DELLO SPORT
S. CROCE
Piazza Apollodoro
Via Guido Reni
FLAMINIO
Piazza Gentile da Fabriano
Viale Flaminio
Viale del Vignola
Piazza Melozzo da Forlì
Villa Flaminia
Via Flaminia
Viale Tiziano
Via Donatello
Via C. Fracassini
Largo A. Sarti
Piazza Maresciallo Giardino
ISTITUTO STORICO E DI CULTURA DELL'ARMA DEL GENIO
Via Gomenizza
Lungotevere della Vittoria
Lung. Flaminio
RAI
Via Durazzo
Via F. Corridoni
Via F. Filzi
Via Timavo
Lung. G. Oberdan
Fiume Tevere
Teulada
Clodia
Angelico
Viale Carso
Via A. Papa
Via Monte Zebio
Via Marcello Prestinari
Piazza Bainsizza
Via Muggia
Via Oslavia
RAI
Piazza Monte Grappa
PONTE D. RISORGIMENTO
Via Dardanelli
Via Monte Santo
CRISTO RE
RAI
Via Pasubio
V. Col di Lana
Via Sabotino
Via P. de' Calboli
Mazzini
Via G. Nicotera
Lungotevere d. Armi
Piazzale Clodio
Piazza G. Mazzini
Viale Giuseppe
Via L. Settembrini
Via C. Menotti
Piazza dei degli Strozzi
Piazza Giovine Italia
Via A. Brofferio
Via G. Ferrari
Via N. Ricciotti
Via A. Mordini
Piazza d. Cinque Giornate
PONTE G. MATTEOTTI
Via Grazioli Lante
Via Silvio Pellico
Via P. Borsieri
Milizie
Via Fornovo
Via Lepanto
Lungotevere Michelangelo
Via G. Bettolo
Viale delle
Via Damiata
Via C. A. Dalla Chiesa
Cesare
LEPANTO
Viale
Via Barletta
Giulio
Via d. Scipioni
SAN GIOACCHINO
V. M. A. Colonna
Via A. Farnese
Via Pompeo Magno
Via dei Gracchi
Piazza della Libertà
OTTAVIANO
Viale
Via Fabio Massimo
Via Paolo Emilio
Piazza dei Quiriti
Via Ezio
Rienzo
Via d. Scipioni
SS.ROSARIO
Via Germanico
Piazza Cola di Rienzo
Via Ottaviano
Via Cola di
Via Tacito
Via Lucrezio Caro
Via E. Q. Visconti
Via F. Cesi
MUSEO STORICO DELL'ARMA D. CARABINIERI
Piazza d. Unità
PRATI
Via Ovidio
Via Boezio
Via Virgilio
Via Cicerone
Piazza del Risorgimento
Via Crescenzio
Leone IV

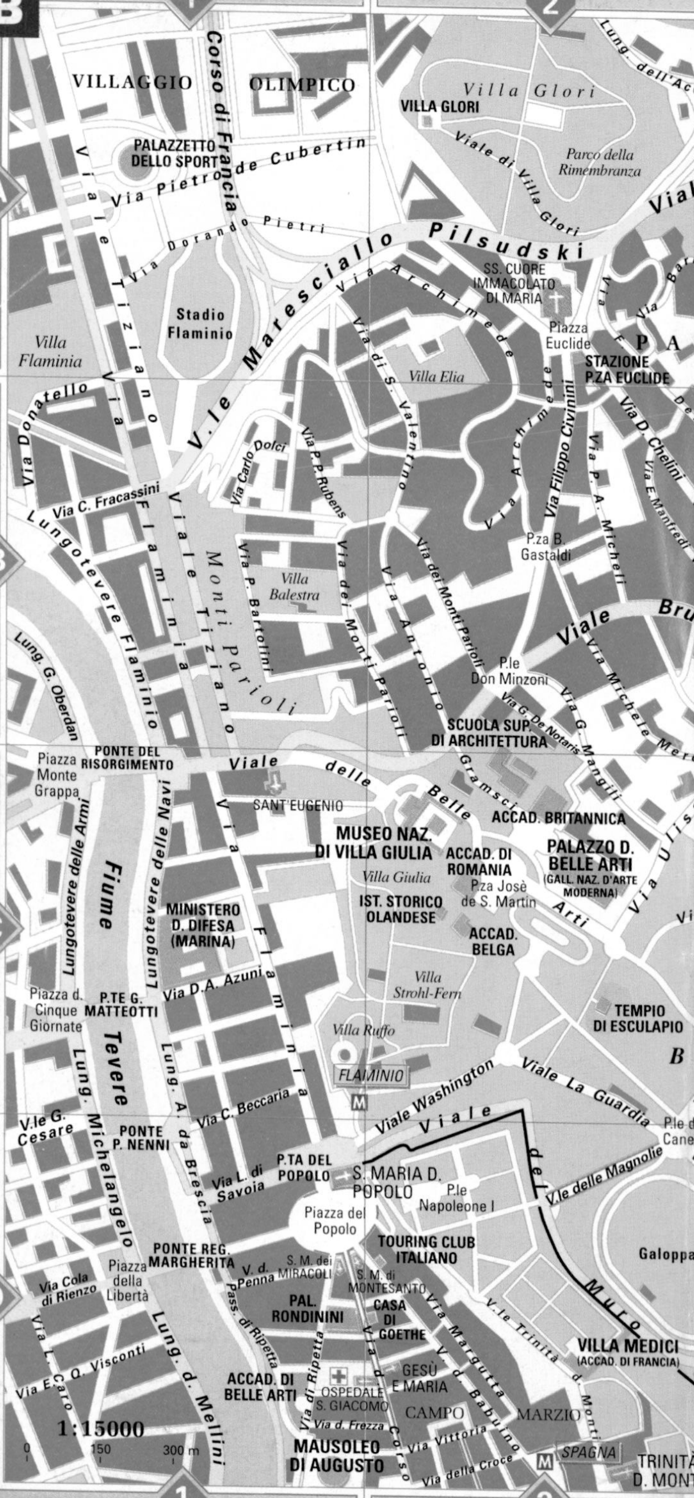
B
1
2
VILLAGGIO
OLIMPICO
Corso di Francia
Villa Glori
VILLA GLORI
Viale di Villa Glori
Parco della Rimembranza
PALAZZETTO DELLO SPORT
Via Pietro de Cubertin
Via Dorando Pietri
Viale Maresciallo Pilsudski
SS. CUORE IMMACOLATO DI MARIA
Piazza Euclide
STAZIONE P.ZA EUCLIDE
Via Archimede
Stadio Flaminio
Villa Flaminia
Viale Tiziano
Via Tiziano
Via Donatello
Villa Elia
Via di S. Valentino
Via Carlo Dolci
Via P.P. Rubens
Via Filippo Civinini
Via D. Chelini
Via E. Manfredi
Via P. A. Micheli
P.za B. Gastaldi
Via C. Fracassini
Lungotevere Flaminio
Flaminia
Monti Parioli
Via P. Bartolini
Villa Balestra
Via dei Monti Parioli
Via Antonio
Viale Bruno Buozzi
P.le Don Minzoni
Via G. De Notaris
Via G. Mangili
Via Michele Mercati
Lung. G. Oberdan
SCUOLA SUP. DI ARCHITETTURA
PONTE DEL RISORGIMENTO
Piazza Monte Grappa
Viale delle Belle Arti
Gramsci
SANT'EUGENIO
ACCAD. BRITANNICA
MUSEO NAZ. DI VILLA GIULIA
Villa Giulia
ACCAD. DI ROMANIA
P.za José de S. Martin
PALAZZO D. BELLE ARTI
(GALL. NAZ. D'ARTE MODERNA)
Via Ulisse
IST. STORICO OLANDESE
ACCAD. BELGA
Lungotevere delle Armi
Fiume
Lungotevere delle Navi
MINISTERO D. DIFESA (MARINA)
Via Flaminia
Villa Strohl-Fern
Via D.A. Azuni
Piazza d. Cinque Giornate
P.TE G. MATTEOTTI
Villa Ruffo
TEMPIO DI ESCULAPIO
Tevere
FLAMINIO
Viale Washington
Viale La Guardia
Lung. A. da Brescia
Via C. Beccaria
Lung. Michelangelo
V.le G. Cesare
PONTE P. NENNI
P.le dei Canestre
Viale del Muro Torto
Via L. di Savoia
P.TA DEL POPOLO
S. MARIA D. POPOLO
P.le Napoleone I
V.le delle Magnolie
Piazza del Popolo
TOURING CLUB ITALIANO
Galoppatoio
PONTE REG. MARGHERITA
Piazza della Libertà
V. d. Penna
S. M. dei MIRACOLI
S. M. di MONTESANTO
Via Cola di Rienzo
PAL. RONDININI
CASA DI GOETHE
Via Margutta
V.le Trinità d. Monti
VILLA MEDICI
(ACCAD. DI FRANCIA)
Lung. d. Mellini
Pass. di Ripetta
Via L. Caro
Via E. Q. Visconti
ACCAD. DI BELLE ARTI
Via di Ripetta
OSPEDALE S. GIACOMO
GESÙ E MARIA
V. d. Babuino
Via d. Corso
CAMPO MARZIO
Via d. Frezza
1:15000
0
150
300 m
MAUSOLEO DI AUGUSTO
Via Vittoria
Via della Croce
SPAGNA
TRINITÀ D. MONTI
A
B
C
D

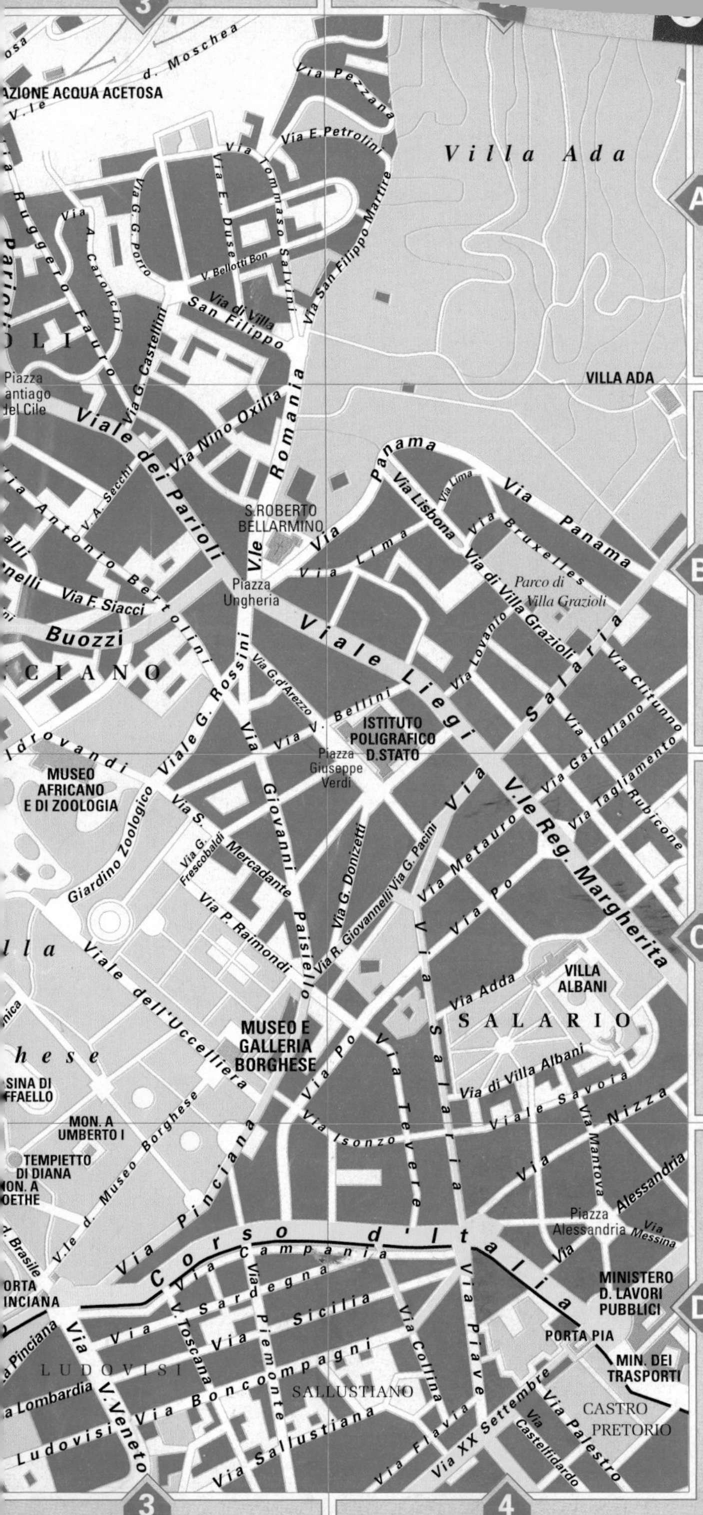

3
Villa Ada
VILLA ADA
A
B
C
D
S.ROBERTO BELLARMINO
Piazza Ungheria
Viale dei Parioli
V.le Romania
Via Panama
Viale Liegi
Via Salaria
ISTITUTO POLIGRAFICO D.STATO
Piazza Giuseppe Verdi
MUSEO AFRICANO E DI ZOOLOGIA
Giardino Zoologico
Viale G. Rossini
Via Giovanni Paisiello
V.le Reg. Margherita
Parco di Villa Grazioli
VILLA ALBANI
SALARIO
MUSEO E GALLERIA BORGHESE
Viale dell'Uccelliera
Via Pinciana
Corso d'Italia
MON. A UMBERTO I
TEMPIETTO DI DIANA
Piazza Alessandria
MINISTERO D. LAVORI PUBBLICI
PORTA PIA
MIN. DEI TRASPORTI
CASTRO PRETORIO
LUDOVISI
SALLUSTIANO
Via V. Veneto
Via Boncompagni
Via Sallustiana
Via XX Settembre
Via Piave
4

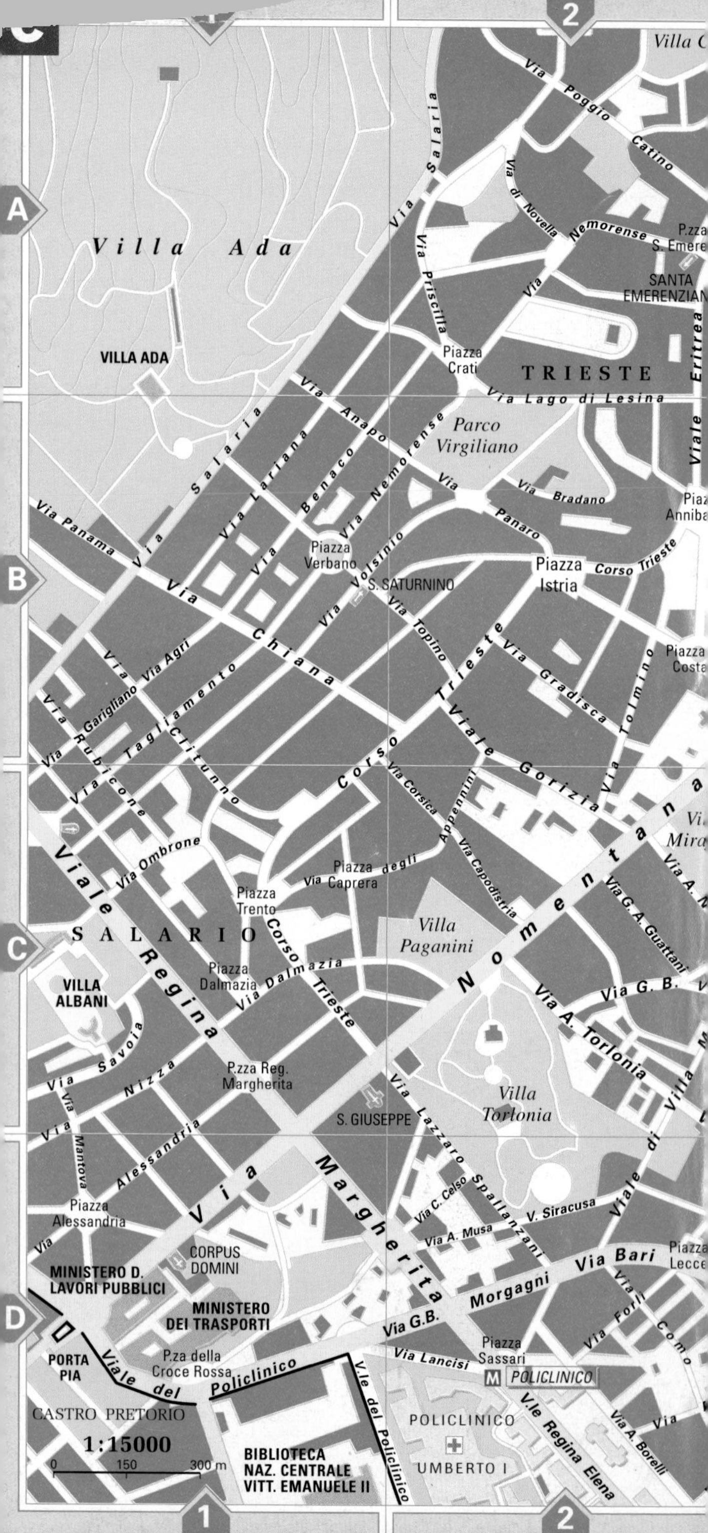

Villa Ada
VILLA ADA
TRIESTE
SALARIO
Parco Virgiliano
Villa Paganini
Villa Torlonia
VILLA ALBANI
SANTA EMERENZIANA
S. SATURNINO
S. GIUSEPPE
CORPUS DOMINI
MINISTERO D. LAVORI PUBBLICI
MINISTERO DEI TRASPORTI
PORTA PIA
CASTRO PRETORIO
BIBLIOTECA NAZ. CENTRALE VITT. EMANUELE II
POLICLINICO UMBERTO I
POLICLINICO
Via Salaria
Via Priscilla
Via di Novella
Via Poggio Catino
Via Nemorense
P.zza S. Emerenziana
Viale Eritrea
Piazza Crati
Via Lago di Lesina
Via Anapo
Via Lariana
Via Benaco
Via Bradano
Via Panaro
Piazza Annibaliano
Piazza Istria
Corso Trieste
Via Panama
Piazza Verbano
Via Volsinio
Via Topino
Via Chiana
Via Agri
Via Garigliano
Via Tagliamento
Via Clitunno
Via Rubicone
Via Gradisca
Via Tolmino
Piazza Costa
Viale Gorizia
Via Corsica
Via Appennini
Via Capodistria
Via Nomentana
Via Ombrone
Piazza degli Appennini
Via Caprera
Piazza Trento
Corso Trieste
Piazza Dalmazia
Via Dalmazia
Viale Regina Margherita
Via G. A. Guattani
Via G. B.
Via A. Torlonia
Via Savoia
Via Nizza
P.zza Reg. Margherita
Via Mantova
Via Alessandria
Piazza Alessandria
Via Lazzaro Spallanzani
Via C. Celso
V. Siracusa
Via A. Musa
Viale di Villa
Via Bari
Piazza Lecce
Via G.B. Morgagni
Via Forlì
Via Como
Piazza Sassari
Via Lancisi
POLICLINICO
Viale del Policlinico
V.le del Policlinico
V.le Regina Elena
Via A. Borelli
P.za della Croce Rossa
1:15000
0
150
300 m
A
B
C
D
1
2